OF THE EAST

Walter A. Fairservis, Jr.

Costumes photographed by Thomas Beiswenger
Drawings by Jan Fairservis

Published in association with
The American Museum of Natural History

The Chatham Press, Inc., Riverside, Connecticut

ACKNOWLEDGMENTS

The author is greatly indebted to Suydam Cutting whose generosity over the years
has made this costume collection possible. Thanks are also due Dr. Stanley Freed,
Avis Kniffin and Lisa Whittall for their work in assembling and cataloging the
collection and their assistance on this book.

SBN 85699-029-0 Clothbound Edition
SBN 85699-029-9 Paperbound Edition
Library of Congress Catalog Card Number: 77-159783

Manufactured in the United States of America. Color separations made by Viking Color Separations,
Inc. of Fairfield, Connecticut, type composed by Darien Phototypographers of Darien, Connecticut,
printed through Printing Corporation of America at Livermore & Knight Co. of Providence, Rhode
Island, and bound by Montauk Book Manufacturing Co. Inc. of Harrison, New Jersey. Paper was
supplied by the S. D. Warren Co.

DISTRIBUTED BY THE VIKING PRESS, INC.

CONTENTS

Introduction 7
I   Costume and the West 13
II The Asian Setting 31
III The Circles of Ethnohistory 40
    CIRCLE A: Balkans, Caucasus, Ukraine..................... 40
    CIRCLE B: Near East 52
    CIRCLE C: Iran (Persia) and Afghanistan 69
    CIRCLE D: Central Asia 73
    CIRCLE E: India and Pakistan 85
    CIRCLE F: The High Borderlands. Kashmir, Nepal, Sikkim, and Bhutan..... 90
    CIRCLE G: Tibet 101
    CIRCLE H: Southeast Asia...................................... 105
    CIRCLE I: China 117
    CIRCLE J: Japan and Korea 121
    CIRCLE K: Southeast Siberia, Manchuria, Hokkaido, and Bonins 131
    CIRCLE L: Siberia 142
Appendix.. 153

INTRODUCTION

The collections from which the material for this book is drawn began with the founding of The American Museum of Natural History in 1869 by individuals who were products of the Victorian Age of Inquiry. Still believing in a man-centered world in which the achievements of Western civilization were regarded as paramount, they nonetheless were motivated by Darwinian concepts to investigate the life of non-Western man. This inclination was coupled with a prime interest in all aspects of natural history, for it was a time when men of education considered natural history and the study of man as one and the same thing. The term *natural philosophy* was used to label this view. But over the next hundred years, The American Museum was to see the separation of the study of man (anthropology) from the study of natural history, with serious consequences to the former in the context of the Museum.

For more than twenty years after The American Museum's founding, an effort was made to acquire artifacts of the prehistoric ages, which were then newly being recognized in Europe. It was also a period in which the Museum accumulated objects that represented cultures of other peoples throughout the world. The obvious emphasis was on the American Indian, but Eurasian material, especially that of China, Japan, and the Turkish Empire, was also obtained. Unfortunately, no particular system was applied to this collecting, for interests in exotica and the curio tended to motivate private collectors whose donations could be prominently seen in the exhibitions of the day.

In the 1890's, the appearance on the Museum staff of Franz Boas, called by some the "father of modern anthropology," thrust the Department of Anthropology into the forefront of that new field. Boas provided The American Museum with a perspective few museums have ever had. He felt that a museum should be "An archive of all which can be obtained of the human condition in time and space." Li-

Detail from an engraving depicting the opening ceremonies of
The American Museum of Natural History which appeared in
Frank Leslie's Illustrated Newspaper, January 5, 1878.

braries, he thought, should preserve the written records while a museum's task was to preserve the tools, weapons, and art; material manifestations of ideas, ideologies, and dreams that are the graphic representations of a total culture. As libraries kept books, so should museums keep and display the artifacts of traditional life for all the generations to come. There was an urgency about Boas's view of The American Museum's role. Even in his time he saw the almost daily extinction of the world's native cultures before the blandishments and coercions of Western civilization. He knew that this course of events would someday spell the end of aboriginal cultures whose study gave vital insights into human conditions that must be understood and preserved if anthropology was to contribute significant knowledge in a world where reason had ascendancy.

One result of Boas's foresight was the Jesup expeditions to the North Pacific region. Morris K. Jesup, a remarkable philanthropist in a period of remarkable philanthropy, thoroughly and materially supported Boas's effort to record the cultures of the North Pacific rim. For almost thirteen years, Museum representatives worked among the aboriginal peoples there. The results can be seen by examining the publications of the Jesup expeditions, as well as by visiting the Museum's Hall of Tribal Life of North Pacific America.

The Jesup expeditions were not confined to the New World, for in Boas's view it was essential to have information about the Asian side of the Pacific Ocean too. Whereas he and his immediate colleagues could concentrate on the New World coasts of Canada and Alaska, Boas found two Russian scholars, Vladimir Jacobsen and W. Bogoras, whose academic interests and experiences qualified them for the onerous task at hand — the recording of aboriginal Siberia. For a dozen years these men studied, lived, and thought in terms of the daily life of an aboriginal people in one of the extreme climatic areas of the world, where the temperature can drop to below -50 degrees Fahrenheit. As a result of their labors, case after case of specimens, accompanied by voluminous documentation, crossed the seas from Vladivostok to New York. Here was a record of the life of Paleo-Asiatic people expressed not only in literary terms but in artifacts. Costumes, tools, weapons, sleds, effigies, tents — all came to New York. These objects depicted — indeed underlined — a way of life at least a millennium old but doomed to perish.

As the collections grew, the Museum administration was confronted by growing problems of physical storage and by an inability to comprehend Boas's position. Eventually, it balked. It was all right to acquire key objects of a culture — the art, for example — but the accumulation in quantity of pots and pans, skin boats, and the plebeian artifacts of daily life was considered meaningless. What the blazes was Boas doing?

The situation reached a climax when the German anthropologist, Berthold

Laufer, was employed by Boas to work in southern Siberia, Japan, and China. A more thorough and catholic man has never existed than Berthold Laufer! He started his work by fulfilling several years of systematic study and collecting among such peoples as the Ainu of northern Japan and the Gilyak and Goldi of the Amur River region. While Laufer worked, Boas published the findings and encouraged him as much as possible. As Laufer moved south into China proper, Boas was instrumental in encouraging the Museum to create a committee on East Asia. "Today's China of the centuries will not exist tomorrow," he said. "If we are to study the phenomenon of civilization, the China of today gives us an unparalleled opportunity." Supported by Boas, Laufer studied and collected. Over 20,000 ethnological specimens representative of Chinese traditional daily life left the ports of China and ended in the storage rooms of The American Museum. Kites, preserved food, herbs, cricket gourds, paintings, pots, ploughs, pails, knives, hats, coats, lacquer, toys, mats, baskets, carts — the list reads like a hardware store inventory. Here was traditional China documented by its artifacts; not as an esoteric exercise of a scholarly commune, but by realistic, tangible evidence of a way of life.

In the end, however, Boas left the Museum. The administrative powers had decided The American Museum of Natural History was to be exactly that — a natural history museum of America. What was American or natural history should be of prime interest to The American Museum of Natural History; the Boas-Laufer emphasis on Asia was therefore not in the Museum's interest. As a result, Asia, Africa, and Europe were not to be emphasized in anthropology. To the administrators, anthropology was not really a science but rather a kind of departmental archive, where things of esoteric interest might reasonably be preserved.

In 1908 came the presidency of Henry Fairfield Osborn, a paleontologist who, in collaboration with N. C. Nelson, a New World archeologist of Scandinavian background, accumulated collections in Old World prehistory that are still exemplary in the United States. Later, in a Hall of Prehistoric Man, the Museum exhibited not only the actual evidence for the cultures of prehistoric man of non-*Homo sapiens* type, but the whole spectrum of knowledge of modern man's remote ancestry. France, Germany, Spain, the Scandinavian countries, central Europe, Hungary, Russia, China, and India were represented in that hall. Moreover, it was the period in which Roy Chapman Andrews was able to convince the Museum administration that exploration of inner Asia had significance for many sciences. Osborn, under the mystique of the "Mother Asia" idea, supported Andrews as Boas had supported Laufer. The Gobi Desert expeditions, like those of Jesup, again thrust the Museum into the forefront of pioneering scientific endeavor in Asia.

The chairmanship of Harry L. Shapiro (1942-1969) was a turning point in the anthropology department's history. Realistically assessing the department's abilities to grow, yet confronted with the exigencies of modern anthropology, Shapiro developed a strategy. He agreed to invest departmental resources selectively into critical anthropological needs, among which was a revival of Boas's plan to archive traditional cultures while one could. Whereas Boas had hoped for a slower degree of acculturation of the modern with the traditional, Shapiro was aware that there were no more than two or three decades left in which to obtain primary source materials from rapidly disappearing ways of life.

Still, Eurasia had to be second best in the context of departmental goals simply because resources were so limited. This had its tragic overtones. While Museum administrations encouraged philanthropy to create new facilities for almost all of the numerous departments, anthropology was largely neglected. Cry out as one might that a decade or two was all that was left in which to salvage invaluable documentation, the effect was largely futile. What was scientific about an old plough or a traditional costume? What had anthropology to contribute compared to the taxonomy of a bird, insect, dinosaur, or fish? No funds were available!

Still, Shapiro encouraged Eurasian researchers wherever he could. Joel Halpern, a graduate anthropologist from Columbia University, was supported in his work in Serbia and Laos; Joan Mencher of similar background received support for work in Indian Kerala and Madras; the author of this book conducted studies in Pakistan and Afghanistan.

By husbanding his resources, Shapiro was able to create one of the finest collections of African ethnology in the world, while at the same time developing the Eurasian collection. Recognizing not only that Siberia and China were areas now closed to American anthropological research, but also that there were already adequate holdings from these areas, Shapiro put what funds he could into the filling of collection gaps. This led to the development of collections from Southeast Asia, India, Arabia, and Turkey. Today the Dentan collection of the Senoi-Semai of Malaysia (unequaled in the world); the Fürer-Hamendorf, Okada, and other collections from the Indian subcontinent and Nepal; Louis Dupree's collections from Afghanistan; Lawrence Krader's from western Iran; and Kenan Erin's from Turkey are all representative of the successes of this exponent of the Boas tradition. Tibetan studies have been somewhat handicapped by too much emphasis on the religious character of that culture. Yet the Museum was able, through the early interest of Laufer, the travels of the philanthropist Suydam Cutting, the curatorship of A. K. Gordon, the contributions of Thubten Norbu, elder brother of the present Dalai Lama, and above all the views of H. L. Shapiro, to create a substantive, documented collection of Tibetan secular and religious life. This, along with the East Asian collection created by Boas, is a durable contribution of inestimable value to the study of man in inner and eastern Asia.

Those who attend the Museum's 1971 exhibition of its costume collection will see but a few examples of what must be considered the most comprehensive collection of Eurasian life in the New World and one of the three or four ranking collections of its kind in the world. This collection has been largely unseen by the public, and is basically unknown even to academia; however, the Museum now plans a new hall of Eurasian peoples for which this particular exhibition is but a sampling. Thanks to the wisdom of a few devoted men, the traditional way of life for many peoples of Eurasia is preserved for all to see.

I

COSTUME AND THE WEST

Some years ago a special exhibition on the arts of ancient Peru was held at The American Museum of Natural History. The lovely, masterful, and infinitely colorful metal, pottery, stone, and fabric objects on display represented the cultures of civilized and aboriginal Peru before the arrival of the white man. The opening of this splendid exhibition was attended not only by representatives of the Museum, the press, and the city, but by members of the social and business elite of New York. The men wore business suits, all cut approximately the same way and made grave by the shades of gray, black, and brown conventional to the modern American male. The ladies, conscious of current fashion, wore dresses differing slightly from one another in cut, but almost all sharing one color — black! Most of these dresses, regardless of design, were adorned by a string of pearls. The appearance of modern man as represented by this sample was funereal and conformist. When one considers how many individuals in this group commanded wealth and power suitable to the ambitions of past monarchs, the factors that created this costuming must, indeed, be stringent. These people, as well as most urbanized citizens of the West, are heirs to that whole colorful tradition of costume that runs from ancient western Asia through Godey's *Ladies Book* to the current French fashion mart. There was, and is, no reason why this incredible resource in history could not be drawn on to produce variety in the costumes of modern man — except for limitations imposed by cultural conventions.

Costume is basic to man's culture, and is as much a part of his natural history as the courtship dance is to the ruffed grouse or social behavior is to the African lion. With its vast variety of form and ornament, costume provides the anthropologist with a graphic choice for sorting out the ethnic, occupational, and social categories to which individuals of the species *Homo sapiens* belong.

Conventions of dress have always been rooted in the value system, in the

Attired in formal dress of Western great tradition, patrons attend the opening of the new Metropolitan Opera House in New York.

technology and economics, and in the communicative aspects of one's culture. Until very recently, whether you worked on Madison Avenue or on New Bond Street, wearing a pair of bright red socks or an emerald green tie to the office might have subjected you to a barrage of disparaging remarks. In some cases, were you to continue such behavior, people might gossip about you — or even make comments about your personal life. Costume deviances have even led to circumstances in which the individual lost his job. While attitudes today are somewhat more relaxed, conformity is still the general rule.

The youth revolt of the 70's is strikingly evident in costume. The T-shirted, dungareed, barefooted, and long-haired young men who may wear African shirts or Asian costume jewelry do so that they may directly contrast with the shirted and tied, neatly coated, panted, shiny-shod, and largely unjeweled establishment exponent of Western cities and towns. Their female counterparts are equally in contrast. Ironically, however, once the rebellious generation establishes its costume conventions, it adheres to them as rigidly as does any other generation. Costume on either side of the generation gap is now so conventional that little of the unexpected is found among whites in either European or American cities. Indeed, Western man appears to have decisively limited his costume repertory to what is efficient, generally drab, and conformist. In part this is due to the mass production of inexpensive clothing, but more important, Western man candidly admits he likes his clothing that way.

One may ask why this is so, for if the present costumes of Western man are the end result of the cultural evolution that created Western civilization (and we have no reason to think that the development of costume is divorced from that evolution), then conformity in modern costume is perhaps symptomatic of conformity on a deeper and more meaningful level. From Moscow to San Francisco most men and women wear the same kind of clothes, varying only slightly from the norm according to occupation or wealth. The Japanese, Chinese, and urbanized inhabitants of Southeast Asia, India, western Asia, and Africa have also seized on this type of clothing. The Australians and most Latin Americans are part of the same clothing picture. All who are involved with modern industrialization and its expression in the production and control of goods and services, whatever their nation, wear the same basic costume.

It is helpful to take a closer look at this basic costume through the eyes of an anthropologist, beginning with undergarments for both sexes. These generally consist of two pieces (undershirt and underpants for men, brassiere and pants for women), except that women usually add a slip. Men put on two pieces of outer clothing (trousers with a zipper or button fly, held up by a belt or, increasingly rarely, by suspenders, and a shirt that buttons in front and has a stiff or semistiff

The youth of Europe and America rebel against the clothing of their elders, yet in turn conform to standards of their peers.

collar). Sometimes a piece of colored cloth, a tie, is suspended from the tightly buttoned collar. Women wear the equivalent of men's garb, generally substituting a skirt for trousers, a blouse with some variation in cut for a shirt, or a one-piece dress for both. The women's pants-suit has also come into vogue and seems set to stay, because of its ease and comfort.

The so-called "suit coat" is worn widely by male white collar workers and by executives of all types; it has its equivalent in the short coats of women. Its advantages are easy removal and abundant pockets. Socks and shoes for men, stockings and often pronouncedly heeled shoes for women, are conventional footwear.

In cold weather, men wear an outer garment. This varies from a calf-length coat to a jacket or sweater that terminates near the belt line. Women similarly wear overgarments, but these have greater variation in both material and cut than their male counterparts. Raincoats are widely used by both sexes.

Men's hats have been decreasing in popularity and seem to be on their way out. Women's hats appear in some variety and are among the most unconventional items in the Westerner's clothing repertory. However, the recent trend in women's hair styles and the use of wigs have contributed to hats being worn less than in the past.

Western costume clearly reflects certain behavioral attitudes of Western man. For example, for men, the more formal the occasion, the more somber the clothing. The highest expression of this habit is seen in the basically black and white tuxedo, or in "tails," which constitutes the most formal costume. For women, the more formal the occasion, the greater is the effort to be distinctively different from other women. On the other hand, the more informal the occasion, the more brightly do men dress.

Social differences among people are generally designated only by marks of wealth: quality of cloth, jewelry, coiffure, etc. Occupational differences are distinguished by uniforms or special dress for policemen, firemen, postmen, conductors, clergy, athletes, and others, or by the daily informal clothes of the laborer compared to the relative formality of the office worker.

Ceremonial occasions marked by specific dress are rare in Western cultures. Weddings where the bride wears a special gown that might even be a hundred-year-old family heirloom are still common, but usually conventional dress suffices for birthdays, funerals, parties, and church. All but heirloom costumes are usually machine-made and tend to wear out rapidly. People obtain new clothes almost on a yearly basis.

Since the Renaissance, Western costume has changed so rapidly that in a history of costume one can chronologically pinpoint almost any costume at will. Looking at Western costume from this historical perspective, two phenomena become apparent. First, until very recently, men's formal dress had become increasingly drab and characterless, with individualism increasingly subordinate to uniformity. Women appear to have widened their costume perspective within the conventional forms described above.

Second, the term *style* — the fashion of dress that is current and has wide acceptance among one's peers — has universally penetrated costume circles. For women of means, style change is apparently motivated by a small fashion elite centered mainly in Paris. From this center are launched yearly style changes, whose success or failure may be judged ultimately on their reception by garment industries in the manufacturing centers such as Manchester and Manhattan. What is styled by an elite for an elite is eventually expressed in mass production for the common people, and is imposed on all wearers of clothes without regard to physique or social status. This is as true for the high school student in the American midwest as it is for the Park Avenue socialite. The recent miniskirt fashion is a case in point. In order to stay in style, women with fat legs went dutifully about in brief skirts that often made them more ludicrous than fashionable. The plum color of legs and thighs, as winter winds had their way with exposed flesh, was a colorful tribute to the tyranny of style.

Men's costume, on the other hand, has no such annual cycle of change and has altered relatively little in the past seventy years. The high collars, vests, cravats, watch pockets, buttoned sleeves, and cuffs of 1900 can still be seen today in men's clothing which, in the West, is largely vestigial to the great ages of male fashions in the eighteenth and nineteenth centuries.

Westerners have generally had only a subdued color consciousness. Even on informal occasions, men have tended to avoid prime colors in their clothes, as have women on formal occasions. Soft hues and subtle tonal coloration were preferred. For most Westerners, prime colors have seemed dangerous. If one wore bright colors, there had to be a firm reason attached to the occasion. Otherwise the individual would be calling attention to himself, and in a conformist society, most people find this markedly out of style.

Western dress has its daily and its seasonal aspects. In America and much of Western Europe the majority of white collar workers change into three costumes each day: the semiformal office costume, an informal at-home costume, and a nightdress or pajama with an overdress called a bathrobe. Dress is also changed to conform with the demands of weather. Since much of Western culture is located in temperate zones where four seasons are experienced, dress may be required to match each.

Western clothes generally allow for efficient robing and disrobing. With the exception of his tie, a man can put on his business suit in less than a minute if he so wishes. A woman can dress almost as fast. In fact, throughout the history of the fashion industry, Western women have always been attracted to new fads, new gadgets, additions and subtractions to their costume to bring more and more efficiency to their dressing. Panty hose is probably today's best example of this.

Male dress, in the West, usually covers the body completely. For women the legs, arms, and lower throat can be exposed even in the office. Tight-fitting clothes for women in which the contours of the body are rather sharply outlined have been conventional in Western Europe and the United States since World War I.

The mass media have had an awesome effect upon Western clothing. The appearance of a movie star or television queen in a new style often creates a demand that returns millions of dollars to the manufacturers. In this sense Western costume is by no means an expression of local custom but of a universalism created through mass media by industry. This is certainly one major factor in developing the conformist character of Western clothing, for what appears in one retail store will appear in another.

We have seen that in Western costume there is little expression of ethnic origin, of social and occupational status, or indeed of aesthetic inspiration. The Westerner is constantly reminded of the need to conform and to stay in style. There is, however, a countercurrent that defies the conformist efforts of the mass producer. Go to the tourist office of any European country and ask for brochures and pictures. Amid the colorful graphic representations of old monuments, geographical splendors, gastronomic emporiums, water and snow playgrounds, and other tourist lures appear pictures of happy people in traditional garb performing in a festival or standing around in an idyllic setting. Here is the old Europe, surviving even today, which each country thrusts at the visitor as if to say "come and see us as we really are." Similarly, the American tourist bureaus are apt to represent the American West by the depiction of Indians and cowboys.

What this actually means, of course, is that no tourist wants to look at the same things he sees at home. Since the tourist trade is so lucrative, countries that long since have deliberately and sometimes maliciously exterminated local customs and beliefs now find themselves eager to revive them, or to preserve what is left, for purely economic reasons. Moreover, Western countries are so increasingly uniform in their modernity that they are hard put to identify themselves visually not only to the outside world, but to their own citizens, without recourse to the traditional images of the past — one of which is local costume.

In the United States, folk societies exist in considerable number, each with the stated objective of preserving the traditions of the ethnic group to which they belong. Thus Polish, Ukrainian, Lithuanian, Russian, Czech, Slovak, Hungarian, German, Irish, Greek, Armenian, Chinese, and many other national groups carry on traditional arts, games, and languages, as well as ceremonies in which original or replicas of ethnic costumes are used.

Because Westernized nations today can identify themselves graphically only through the use of old symbols, the study of the phenomenon of costume is particularly important. What is "costume" anyway? It certainly is not simply clothing.

Blacks in America who seek identity for themselves, not as descendants of slaves, patronized or obstructed by whites in the modern world, but as a people with proud roots in the traditions of Africa, often express this historical identity by adopting African hair styles, African jewelry, and of course African clothing, particularly that of West Coast Africa. Even more striking is their display of prime colors and "loud" patterns in their Western clothing, which whites — establishment or rebel — generally avoid. Exaggerations of Western clothing are also inspired by blacks, such as in the "zoot suit" fad of the 1940's that arose from black communities in New Orleans and New York. Today the marvelous and often bizarre exaggeration of the clichés of white male apparel proclaim as much as any other symbol, and more than most, the identity of the black "brother." It is striking that black male costume has undergone this development, while black female dress has more often tended to be an adaptation of truly African clothing rather than altered Western dress, though even when this is the case, special ornamentation plays an important role in establishing the identity of the wearer.

The motivation for or against a certain kind of costume is rooted ultimately in the subconscious. It is a part of man's psychological urge to be identified as a member of a group, both as an individual contributing to that group and as an exponent of the cohesiveness of the group. The refusal of a child to wear what his parents wish him to wear is largely motivated by fear of rejection by his peers or by concern that his costume may cast him in an unsuitable role. Clearly, he who deviates from the costume of the group represents something to which the group must react, whether it be in terms of respect, admiration, obedience, or love, or in terms of derision, humiliation, ostracism, or hatred. As with all symbols, the symbol user expects, or should expect, those who are affected by the symbol to be motivated to an action of some kind. No one is neutral to the symbols of his culture.

The history of costume demonstrates this concern with identity, but it also expresses another aspect of the psychology of the individual. All cultures have a place for the expression of individual achievement. Successful individuals gain privileges, rewards, and the opportunity to display the symbols of their achievement. To wear such symbols is to express pride and to have, almost paradoxically, both a place within the group and special status above it. For example, in Korea certain clothes forbidden to younger men are worn by old men as symbols of their achievement upon reaching retirement after years of faithful adherence to duty. Chinese scholars wore certain honored robes according to academic status. Today, even in the West, university faculty wear various hoods and gowns at formal occasions to distinguish their academic achievements. The medals of military men and the jackets of Olympic teams are in this same category. Here costume enhances the status of the individual.

Just as costume is affected by the special nature of the wearer, so can the wearer be affected by the nature of the costume. In the theater there are two basic approaches to acting, often overlapping but still antithetical. The "inner" approach is concerned with the psychological or empirical reasons why a character behaves as he does, and from this understanding flows automatically, as in life, the qualities that motivate the stage action. The "outer" approach places the actor in the midst of the physical properties vital to the action. From these flow the motivation necessary to the characterization. "Place a man of feeling in a hussar's uniform and he will move like a hussar." It is this second approach in the art of acting that is closest to, and often identical with, the role of costume in the behavior of the individual. If one is conscious of the meaning of what one wears, one restricts or expands one's self accordingly. Military men realize the importance of respect for the uniform in motivating civilian recruits to behave like soldiers. Because the soldier's uniform is a symbol of courage, it requires all who wear it to have courage. Another example is the costume party, which allows the individual to assume for a short time qualities that he does not normally express or represent. Indeed, he may find an outlet for the expression of emotions that must be suppressed in other situations; costume in this regard can be as heady as alcohol.

Costume is unique to man. But why do men wear clothes? Overall dress may have evolved as *Homo sapiens* lost his presumed hirsuteness toward the end of the Pleistocene, or as his peregrinations brought him from warmer climes to more Arctic ones. But man is wonderfully adaptive biologically, and there is no reason to believe that he could not have retained relative or absolute nudity through natural selection under different climatic conditions. Was it, then, a sense of modesty that led to clothing? This is a question we shall probably never be able to answer. If we are to understand some of the attitudes toward sex today, we must draw the inference that "the body is beautiful, and clothes are ugly." If we are to accept this belief, we apparently must also accept the fact that throughout the history of civilization with its varied and complex clothing styles, man has tried to deny his body, the most important natural aesthetic symbol available to him. In part this is probably true, but only in part, since, as has been suggested above, costume is more than mere covering.

It is possible that the first clothing was worn simply to protect the genitalia and other vulnerable areas of the body. The genitalia of both sexes and the female breasts are highly sensitive; a blow or scratch in those areas is painful and can be incapacitating. Thus it would seem sensible for man to provide artificial protection for those parts of the body. Furthermore, even among surviving aboriginal peoples both the excretory and menstrual functions are regarded as antisocial. Concealment of the organs of such functions appears to be the result of this attitude.

Critical to our understanding of the character and role of costume is, of course, man's attitude toward sex. It has been said that costume should be regarded not as the concealer of one's sexual character, but rather as its revealer. Too many in the West regard the genitalia, rather than the men or the women who possess them, as the symbols of sex. Oddly, as students of erotica well know, the simple exposure of genitalia is not as erotic as the partly clothed body. The difference between the sexes is not simply a matter of plumbing, but in its ideal sense, a matter of the whole person who possesses a form of body and a state of mind that complement or supplement the opposite sex. It is a mutuality that transcends biological identity and yet in its fullest expression emphatically identifies the individual as a woman or man. One's culture determines what is masculine and feminine by a whole pattern of attitudes and behavioral emphases that are by no means identical from culture to culture.

All this suggests that the development and enhancement of those traits that graphically distinguish maleness and femaleness have been critical to *Homo sapiens.* Certainly, ideals of beauty have an important role. Body painting, tattooing, sweet scents, athletic or dance exhibitions, vocal expression, and the wearing of flowers or certain pelts of animals have been among the graphic enhancers of one's sexual identity. Costume was, and is, a firm supporter of this identity. The recent vogue among Western women for men's clothing may be a part of woman's drive for parity with men!

Whatever the early social forms of man, whether band or tribe, identification of one's group through graphic representation is so commonplace among all peoples, past and present, that we can assume it was a part of prehistoric life. Costume, whether in terms of horned headdresses, painted skin robes, or decorated fur pieces, certainly had a function. We are also aware of specialization in prehistoric times that separately recognized hunters, shamans, and chiefs. We have evidence also that bone and stone necklaces, shell beadwork, and cryptic badges made of varied materials communicated status to the group.

The Eurasian and North African regions saw the beginnings of civilization in the later part of the fourth millennium B.C. These early civilizations of Western Asia and Egypt were heirs to rich weaving traditions that were already at least five thousand years old. In Neolithic remains from Anatolia, Syria, Palestine, Iran, Mesopotamia, and Egypt, we have evidence of the existence of spindles and primitive vertical and horizontal looms. A variety of plant fibers, such as flax, as well as animal hair were spun and woven, and dyeing seems to have been on the scene as early as 6000 B.C. The woven cloth was basically used to wrap around or drape the body. This elementary yet practical form has characterized garments of the Mediterranean, North African, Western and Southern Asian regions until comparatively recent times. Early and elaborated expression of it can be seen in the arts of ancient Egypt and Western Asia.

Wool production seems to have had its genesis in the Anatolian plateau and adjacent hill regions perhaps as early as 2000 B.C. Trade in raw wool and wool cloth was one of the economic essentials of such significant civilizations as Crete, Mycenae, the Old Testament Hebrews, classical Greece, and Rome. ·

Cotton became important in the ancient Mediterranean world only after 500 B.C. Its cultivation seems, on present evidence, to have begun around 2000 B.C. in India, where to this day it is one of the most important products. It was Egyptian cotton, however, that became the desideratum for later Europeans; the Nile Valley is especially suited to the growth of the long-fibered variety that is best for weaving.

The origins of silk are obscure. Traditionally, sericulture has been ascribed to China where evidence for it as early as 1500 B.C. seems well-founded. However, recent archeological discoveries in India have produced evidence for silk cultivation at almost the same date, while its origin in Southeast Asia, another traditional seat for sericulture, is archeologically still mostly unknown. Nevertheless, China's use and refinement of silk from at least the Chou Dynasty onward made her preeminent.

Tailored clothing appears in the historical record from about 2000 B.C., but it probably emerged earlier than that, as the sewn skin robes of the late Stone Age in Europe suggest. However, to both central Asian pastoralists and Arctic hunters, pants and sleeved shirts had obvious advantages over the draped garments of the more southerly peoples. Pants allow for the free movement of the legs while insulating the flesh from weather and wear.

Thus we find that by the time of Christ, the peoples of the Mediterranean world, the Near East, India, and China wore varieties of draped clothing, skirts, pullovers, and wraparounds, while the peoples of central Asia and Europe beyond the Mediterranean realms wore varieties of pants and skirts. The latter group made their clothing largely of wool and animal hair; the former used cotton, linen, and silk. Not that these softer materials were rejected by the people of Europe and central Asia; they were too difficult to obtain since they had to be imported. But there was also another, perhaps equally basic, reason.

Both the ancient Egyptians and the Chinese had strong feelings about wool. Those who wore that rough material were regarded as "barbarians" outside the pale of civilization. In turn there are records of Europeans and central Asians contemptuously remarking on the effeminate silken clothes of "civilization." To have a beard and to wear wool was to be a barbarian or a bandit in the eyes of the Chinese.

To wear silk and be clean shaven was to be weak and unmasculine in the opinion of the Turk. In such ways clothing marked the cultural affinity of people in ancient times. The idea that draped clothing is effeminate and tailored clothing masculine is still found in such remarks as the one supposedly typical of a family dispute: "Who wears the pants in this family, you or I?"

The history of Western costume is comparatively well-known and can be found in many fine books. What is apparent in these histories is the rapid change in the costume of the European elite almost century by century. The costume of the peasantry, which formed the largest portion of the population, changed slowly — until the nineteenth century. Anthropologists recognize two complementary traditions in civilization: a "great tradition" carried by the overriding national and usually urban institutions, such as government, church, the military, and business, and a "little tradition" expressed through local traditions and beliefs — often referred to as the folk order. Folk orders tend to be conservative, and consequently preserve elements of cultural styles for an astoundingly long time. For example, words of the vernacular Latin of ancient Rome were still spoken among certain peasant communities in the Tyrol until recent times. Some European folk art, resistant to the great traditions of more sophisticated European expression, preserves elements of the medieval or primitive world from which it sprang. Until the late nineteenth century, it was possible in much of Europe to detect precisely regional folk allegiances and affinities by observing the distinctive and often colorful costumes of the peasantry. Histories of Western costume justifiably tend to ignore the little tradition in presenting their story, for all too little is known about the costume of the folk order. While the everyday costumes of the peasantry were generally designed for ease of movement required by farming, and were correspondingly simple and utilitarian, the clothing worn for church, for festivals, or for weddings, styled by centuries of tradition, was colorful and locally distinctive. Such costumes can be seen in the folk museums of Europe and, rarely, on festival occasions in a few "unspoiled" sections of that continent. However, this does not mean that the local tradition of costume is nearly dead, for among the many ethnic groups of Europe that still claim a degree of autonomy, costume has nationalist meaning. Indeed, even exponents of the great tradition will use certain characteristic local costume clichés in claiming national identity — as in the tourist folders. Thus, the Tyrolean feathered hat, the Bavarian *lederhosen*, the French beret, the Dutch cap, and the Russian shirt leave little doubt in the viewer's mind as to what nation is involved.

The finest folk costumes were made at home or by the best seamstresses in the village or district. They were prized possessions which were always carefully stored, cleaned and mended. Often the combination of intricate sewing, painstaking work, and pride in the result produced a work of art as precious, or indeed more precious, than the products of the weavers' guilds in the courtly cities. Such costume treasures were characteristic of much of Europe's folk culture. Into the creation of these costumes were fed the traditional symbols, the colors, and the iconography that marked the folk belief and gave meaning to the end result. When a peasant girl appeared in her traditional costume, she emphasized her pride in tradition and her identity with it. It was local tradition that made possible her creation and her individuality; her costume was her assurance of membership in the group and her insurance that she could communicate meaningfully within the group. What she wore, when she wore it, and what she did while wearing a given costume derived from centuries of tradition — not in a stultifying sense (for the pragmatic peasantry rarely burdened itself for long with the stiff collars, high pantaloons, and agonizing corsets that the aristocracy forced itself to endure in history) but in a very personal and often mystical sense. What one wore reflected the spirit of the past, the reality of the present, and the hope of the future — a future that would see one's children doing the same things as the parents. It is this personal, tradition-bound quality that marks folk culture generally and that has to be understood if one is to ascertain the true motivation for folk costume. In sum, then, folk costume shows wide variation in its geographic spread, but historically it is conservative and resistant to change. Thus it is more fitting to write histories of folk costume from an ethnographical, rather than a chronological, viewpoint.

The personal and the traditional characteristics of the little tradition are in marked contrast to the impersonal and style-conscious character of the great tradition. The bewildering changes in the history of Western costume reflect the political, social, and economic fortunes of the elite and their supporters. Class consciousness, individual accomplishment, patriotism, wealth, and occupation strongly influence members of the institutions of the great tradition. One can detect the concern of the time in costume development, from the wealthy ostentation of the Renaissance courts through the imperial classicism of the Napoleonic era to the stamped-out conformity of the twentieth century. International contacts, political events, a theatrical personality, war, the state visit of a dignitary, the automobile, a new dance — all have contributed to changes of costume style. The plethora of Asian- or African-derived fashion elements, which the Westerner has eagerly placed in his costume repertory and as eagerly discarded when "out of style," bewilders the mind: *burnooses, turbans, kimonos, saris*, Tartar hats, caps, pajamas, sandals. Napoleon revived the styles of ancient Rome — and some famous personages wore togas; while late in the nineteenth century Donizetti's opera, "Daughter of the Regiment," put fashionable women into fashionable uniforms. The discovery of Tutankhamen's tomb in 1922 had American women dressing like Nefertiti; Walt Disney produced " Davy Crockett" and coonskin caps swept the nation. Beau Brummell, Greta Garbo, Tarzan, Grace Kelly, the Beatles, and many others have caused widespread costume change.

Not all the costumes of the great tradition change as rapidly, however. The Christian Church, with its rich roots in the ancient and medieval world, preserves its continuity with the past in its vestments, as does Judaism in its robes. The English law courts, the German chimney sweeps, and the uniforms of numerous elite guards in various nations still reflect their traditions. And military uniforms demonstrate a history of their own. The factors that govern their character are varied. Outstanding, however, is the need to handle efficiently the tactical weapons of the time. The Napoleonic wars, with their emphasis on the draft of the entire able-bodied male population and the mass movement of armies, constituted one of the most influential periods in the history of military costume. Until that time, great individuality in the uniforms of officers and the various ranks of noncommissioned cadre was prevalent in national, princely, and ducal armies. After Napoleon, variety in uniform was confined mostly to units of regimental rank. These uniforms reflected the role in battle; chasseurs, hussars, dragoons, artillerymen, the infantry, and the like. At the same time, since military units were traditionally derived from given regions within the realm, the uniforms might also reflect that origin. The bewildering variety of uniforms in the K.U.K. Armee of Austria-Hungary in Emperor Franz Joseph's day, for example, represented the bewildering variety of peoples that made up that colorful empire. Insistence upon conformity in uniform in such armies paradoxically contrasted with insistence that regimental variety be emphasized. Thus the Bosnian, Hungarian, Czech, Polish, and various Austrian regiments could be identified at a glance. Indeed, this also reflected a military need to identify quickly a unit in battle. However, as has been noted above, the overriding factor in deciding the character of the military uniform is the technology of weaponry. The dashing mustachioed, jingling, and becaped hussar had to give way to the dun-colored menace of the modern soldier whose individualism, through practical necessity, fell victim to the machine.

Oddly, the Western theater and its adjuncts, the dance and the circus, have been a relatively conservative element in the costumery of the great tradition. Until Ibsen, the theater dealt mainly with historical plays in which conscientious efforts were made by designers to adhere faithfully to historical truth and traditional forms. Clowns, acrobats, and ballet dancers all have traditional dress by which they are known. More recently, social drama, with its de-emphasis of proscenium theater and stage sets, has made contemporary dress (or undress) the actor's costume. Even when historical or traditional plays are given, the designer may use modern dress instead of historical costume.

The history of Western costume is thus one of change within the great tradition

The rapid change in Eurasian costume is illustrated by compar-
ing the Western dress of commuters in modern Japan, at left,
with the clothing worn at a Korean cattle market, above, photographed by Roy Chapman Andrews in 1912.

and of relatively little change within the folk order. At present the folk order is yielding before the massive assault of modern industrialization and its spokesmen, the mass media. National states who link their future to standardization at every level, to the conditioning of their citizenry to one body of laws, to one political theme, to one educational philosophy, and to mass values regard the folk order as not only backward but inconceivable in an age when jets span the earth and rockets reach the moon. So resentful of the folk order are national states that deliberate efforts are made to undermine its hold by subverting its youth, "modernizing" its traditions, and deriding its faith. National states thus obtain their goal — one nation, one people, one government, one belief, and of course one costume repertory. The exponents of change through time overwhelm the exponents of tradition. As pointed out earlier, Western costume is covering the earth.

This conformity of appearance, with its roots in conformity of culture, confronts Asian people as they look to the West and accept Western ways. The almost infinite and kaleidoscopic variety of Asian cultures is already being extinguished by the massive onslaught of the West. China, for example, once one of the most varied and colorful of all Asian cultural forms, is now one of the most conformist and colorless of Asian cultures. And if the present governments of India and Iran have their say, cheap machine-made cloth and national "cottage" industry styles will be the manifest destiny of every wardrobe, regardless of its owner's belief, his cultural heritage, or his income. This in the very lands from which sprang the splendors of design and craftsmanship that have ennobled mankind since early civilizations arose there thousands of years before the first smokestack darkened the skies of the West. The costumes of Asian people will be like those of the West as this trend continues: rapid change in terms of style; while in terms of space, of region, of ethnic origin, only conformity — fashionable as it may be.

As suggested previously, costume is as essential a part of a man's culture as his language, his family, or his occupation; it reflects his identity. But in the conformist world that the West has created, costume is losing its essential place. For if a man is merely a member of an institution, a cog in a great wheel that he must serve from birth to death, what need costume do except confirm his conformity? In that situation, costume is a mere covering, efficiently shaped to the body of a man or woman.

A cartoon published in Vienna recently showed two American tourists in the Great Hall of Schönbrunn, that palace of Hapsburg splendor. Here beneath the glittering chandeliers, surrounded by the aura cast by imperial gold and white, in a place of silent music, a man and his wife, dressed in their "business" suits of brown, gazed about. "These people had no taste," said the man, and his drably dressed wife nodded eager agreement. It wasn't the caption that caught the imagination of the reader; it was that the tourists' costumes were out of place. The Great Hall had been conceived and executed as an imperial seat; a place where the monarch could be seen as he should be seen, in regal costume surrounded by those whose role in life was the service of the monarchy. "My king is splendid as a king should be," says the guardsman and thus confirmed, gladly undertakes the risks of war. The court dress, the uniforms, the manners, and the formality molded into an aesthetic whole with the architecture, which was conceived as being complete only when the costumed court was present.

Whether one is dealing with an imperial palace, a Gothic church, or a football stadium, the costume of people is as much a part of the architectural scheme as the ornament on the wall or the capital on the pillar. It is impossible to obtain the full aesthetic impact of the interior and often the exterior of buildings without the presence of people costumed as the artist knew them.

The great centerpieces of the baroque table, the portrait in the baronial hall, the staircase along whose ascending sides statues pondered the ages, were all part of a conception of beauty that included the living, caparisoned in the costume style that completed the picture. The visitor to such buildings today can only gape and mutter his praise or his gripe about them, for unless he has the imagination of a Ruskin or a Robert Edmond Jones he can only see the torn part of the aesthetic whole — made even more woeful by his own incongruity.

Massive projects in public housing, get-rich-quick land developers, the business-man's and the politician's aesthetics, the need to pour out architects to satisfy in con-crete and steel the demand for structures of "practical function," the automobile, the new arrogance of men who require that nothing be above their intellectual grasp, all these have produced the face of the modern city. Every new building, whether it be a suburban home, a theater, or a new office building, has one premise, coined in a single sentence: "Get the job done." The aesthetics of this premise are aimed at noninterference with the work at hand, whether sleeping, conferring, or typing. Hence the cry for "lots of light" but "not too much," or "art, but nothing disturbing." French Impressionist painting, the circus colors of a Rouault, or the dabs of a Jackson Pollock don't disturb — they blend as does the metal sculpture now prevalent in skyscraper gardens or in the foyers of palaces of culture. In such a world, costuming is indeed part of an aesthetic whole. But it is a whole that can be shattered by the appearance of a black person dressed in the garb of Africa or an Indian lady in her sari, for attention to the individual is not part of modern Western man's idea of beauty.

Costume has been a vibrant part of man's being. It has been an extension of self, a symbol of achievement or failure, a matter of pleasure or pain. Above all, costume has been the individual's expression of himself in the aesthetic whole of his culture. The costumes that enhanced his wife's femininity or his own masculinity, reflected his ancestors' belief in themselves, or enabled him to appear at ease before his peers were more than simple pieces of cloth, for they identified and reinforced the role of the individual.

As Western man tries to develop that which he labels "undeveloped" or "emerging," he slaughters native cultures by the dozens. In India, native craftsmen burn the wood blocks that their ancestors used to print cotton, while in Turkey and Egypt young men laugh at the *fez,* which for centuries symbolized the pride of their ancestors in being an Egyptian or Turk, and then dutifully place the fedoras of the West on their progressive heads. The Soviet Union proclaims the fact that their country is made up of many nations, but throughout those lands Western costume predominates, proclaiming the same imperial arrogance that the United States evokes with the American Indian — "Native costume is good for tourism, but wear it and you are representative of a backward people."

As surely as modern man's machines pollute the environment, so does his costume pollute the aesthetics of the world. This is a crisis as serious as the upsetting of our physical ecology, for only the continued existence of the aesthetic realm will make life worth living. In this realm, one person's or one culture's idea of beauty is not commensurate with the whole of mankind. Yet nature has given man a universal aesthetic principle of which all sensitive men and women are aware — namely, that living in harmony with the landscape is the natural requirement of the whole man. This principle means that the natural world is beautiful and that to live in harmony with it man must be beautiful, too. Beauty involves such qualities as variety, harmony, and individual dignity. It requires beauty of mind and body — the perpetual search of thinking people. For living man, this is expressed not only in action but in appearance. The great hope of the earth is that the proponents of Western culture can be made to consider not only the vulnerability of the physical earth but the mortality of man's cultures. The reality of this mortality is made graphic in man's costume.

II

THE ASIAN SETTING

Where does Asia begin? Where does it end? The line of the Ural Mountains and the Strait of the Dardanelles have traditionally marked the boundary between Western Asia and Eastern Europe. But the demarcation has no real cultural, linguistic, or historical validity. Asia and Europe are as intrinsically bound together culturally as they are topographically. The term *Eurasian* describes the character of many of the cultural forms of Europe and Asia more accurately than *European* or *Asian.* Yet, there is an entity called *Asia* and one called *Europe,* and each has its own character.

To the European, Asia has traditionally meant adherence to introspective religion, unchanging ways, incredible craftsmanship, untold wealth, toiling land-bound peasantry, fatalism, curious writing and literature, romance, absolute rule, and physical boundlessness. To the Asian, Europe has represented the reverse of almost every one of these qualities. And changed as the world has become, there still remains in the consciousness of the European and his offshoot, the American, a romanticized dream of Asia. In contrast to this dream, Mao Tse-tung and other leaders of the "new Asia" may proclaim their "Asianness," but the new Asia has largely risen because of the determination of Asians to use the philosophies and the technologies of the West — the new Asia's dream.

This amalgam of East and West that so characterizes the present makes the identification of Asian and European cultures all the more difficult. One is compelled to look to the past to make precise cultural definitions. Yet this backward look, necessary for purposes of taxonomy, does not perceive fossils; what is defined still has vitality today. Terms such as *German, Cossack,* or *Tibetan* refer not only to present-day peoples, but also to their cultural entities, which are given historical meaning and identity through contrast with other cultures.

The Eurasian land mass — the largest such mass on the planet — has certain

Peasant women of Thailand, above, and Russia, opposite.

overall physical features that have played vital roles in human history. These features have set bounds to man's activities and influenced his character. The most obvious feature is the almost continuous line of mountains, running along an east-west axis, that divides Eurasia into northern and southern halves. Ranges such as the Pyrenees, Alps, Carpathian, Taurus, Caucasus, Elburz, Hindu Kush, Pamir, Karakoram, Himalaya, and Altai make this division in no uncertain terms. Passes or areas where the mountain chain is broken have been points of immense strategic importance to the history of man.

South of these mountains, the climate is generally warm and the terrain often arid. The Mediterranean Sea and the Indian monsoons ameliorate this situation and help to provide the moisture that makes possible an ever increasing population density. North of the chain, the climate is colder and the source of moisture is generally the western ocean, from whence come cyclonic, rain-bearing winds that sustain the vast grassland belt stretching almost continually from Manchuria and the Amur River region to the Danube gate at Vienna. Confined between the great coniferous forests *(taiga)* to the north and the mountains to the south, this "corridor" is a natural link between East and West.

Mainland China outflanks the mountain chain on the east, where the Himalayan Nan Shan group bends dramatically to the south to form the backbone of Southeast Asia. Even in China, however, the region south of the Yangtze River is mountainous and gives a geographic specificity to north and south China proper. Similarly France, the Low Countries, and part of western Germany lie west of the central mass of the Alps and thus outflank it. Separation of both this European region and China from the polarization created elsewhere in Eurasia by the mountain divide yielded unique and immensely important cultural developments.

Just off both shores of the land mass lie the island groups of the British Isles and Japan. The physical situation of both these groups provided strategic isolation, but their proximity to the mainland also permitted contact.

South of the mountains are those lands in which ancient civilization had its origin and its seat. The term *civilization* as used here refers to the establishment of cities in which nonsubsistence-producing populations function through an exchange of goods and services fostered by such specialists as craftsmen, merchants, priests, officials, and rulers. In Western Asia, the Sumerian civilization of the late fourth millennium B.C. culminated in a cultural form that had as its roots five thousand years of interacting, innovative, and dynamic cultural activity. Through these centuries man arose from a cultural style based on prehistoric hunting and gathering to one in which a sedentary life, rooted in agriculture and mercantilism, was the harbinger of civilization. Civilization's accomplishments spread and gathered up indigenous cultures that were often well en route to civilization. Thus by 1500 B.C.,

Egypt, Crete, India, and China had developed civilized cultures. This was also a time when pastoralism had spread to the grasslands beyond the mountains and was being accepted there by mobile tribes. Many of these tribes were to move across the mountains to conquer, to be assimilated by nearby civilizations, or to create new ones in new regions. And so a pattern was set that has characterized the story of civilization up to our modern era.

The search for sources of raw material, increased trade, and new markets formed another pattern in the relationship of civilizations to lands north of the mountains. Eventually civilization itself spread beyond the mountains to develop the dynamic characteristics that in the end gave it world dominance. The last to receive civilization were the British Isles and Japan, yet these lands gave civilization a new dynamic expression that had worldwide consequences. The clash of the Japanese with the British in Asia during World War II marked the end of a long historical and cultural process begun on the shores of the Tigris and Euphrates rivers.

These historical patterns of movement and activity by men of the Eurasian land mass give us a means of ascertaining what is Asian and what is European in the traditional sense. By the time of the Romans, civilization had divided into two specific kinds: Western, which is speculative, dynamic, urban, monotheistic, and innovative; and Eastern, which is nonspeculative, contemplative, conservative, rural, and polytheistic. These civilized entities polarized the cultures of Eurasia. India and China tended toward an exclusiveness that created remarkably unique cultural forms, yet admitted some traits of foreign derivation. At the western end of Asia, Islam arose as an Asian manifestation of the Judeo-Christian heritage adopted by Western civilization as a fundamental of its ideology. In spite of this heritage, Islam evolved into a fully Asian ideology not unlike that of the Chinese and the Indian in character and effect. We therefore find three major centers in Asia proper — Islamic Western Asia, Hindu-Buddhist India, and Confucian China — sharing typically Asian qualities. These centers, in turn, had major effects upon the cultures surrounding them. Oddly, even at the heart of these great centers of Asian culture, primitive groups survived in remote pockets, often practicing ways of life seemingly unchanged since the millennia before Christ. The Islamic tradition, however, like the Christian West, has been typically intolerant of such subgroups, in contrast to India, for example, where primitive people still survive. It is striking that great cultural diversity exists in India and Indian-influenced areas today, while both the Islamic areas and Christian West possess nowhere near such diversity.

South of the mountains and flanking them in the west and east, Islamic Western Asian, Hindu-Buddhist Indian, Confucian Chinese, and Western Christian civilizations held sway traditionally. Beyond the mountains both to the north and on the flanks, pastoral peoples moved from one pole of influence to another, de-

pending on the prevailing strength and aura of the political and economic power of nearby civilizations. Some groups, such as the Huns and the Mongols, came under the influence of at least three of the four main Eurasian civilized centers.

The Christian and Islamic spheres tended to have the greatest influence beyond the mountains because of their aggressive attitudes, including forcible conversion of the nonbeliever and imperial appropriation of their lands. Both the Indian and Chinese civilizations have had aggressive periods, but their territorial ethnocentrism has reduced their direct influence much beyond their own frontiers. India itself fell before the Muslims and the British, while the Chinese, reacting to colonialism, fell before the Western philosophy of Marxism, much as pagan Rome fell before Christianity.

The greatest clash of Asian and European civilizations occurred between Islamic Asia and Christian Europe. This struggle lasted for centuries and had profound effects upon both. Islam made a deep penetration into Spain and Eastern Europe, while Christian Europe eventually obtained control for a time over the Near East. In considering these two civilized entities, one has the greatest difficulty defining where Asia ends and Europe begins; thus the inclusion of Balkan and Ukrainian costume in this book.

Lesghins from the Caucasus, right and Mongols, opposite, photographed early in the twentieth century.

The line between great tradition and little, or folk, tradition is not as clearly defined through costume in Asia as it is in Europe. This seems odd, in view of the vast peasantry that makes up the sedentary backbone of such civilizations as India and China. China, however, has always been one of the most centralized of the world's cultures and its governmental "style" has reached deeply into the villages. In contrast to China, India's great tradition has been characterized by much parochialism in the villages, and little traditions have been apparent everywhere.

Europe has been more like India than China in this regard, for only recently have local "styles" been imperiled by Europe's great tradition. One hundred years ago the European political scene encompassed many small autonomous or semi-autonomous states. Only Russia, Austria, France, Spain, and England were of any significant size, and even here at least token recognition of local identities was made. Such old states as Courland, Burgundy, Wales, Cornwall, and Castile were named in the monarch's titles and marked in his heraldic arms. Germany and Italy were a hodgepodge of minor states, while the Austrian Empire tried to build strength out of its heterogeneity. Most of these small states were proud of their autonomy and the consequent identity of their citizens. Nationalist propaganda of the nineteenth and twentieth centuries, with its emphasis upon a united Italy, Germany, Russia, Poland, Belgium, or Great Britain, rode roughshod over the aspirations of small states, in some cases extinguishing them, in others arousing stronger feelings for self-identity. Thus, the Tuscans of Italy have died as a national force, while the Basques and Walloons have grown in their determination to rule their own destinies. France destroyed Burgundy, but Wales and Scotland proclaim their identity. One of the saddest acts in history was the unification of the German states under Prussia. It led to two wars, the annihilation of old Europe, and the division of new Europe into Russian and American camps. As for Bavaria, Saxony, Württemberg, Hanover, Hesse, and the rest, their citizens' identity has been lost except in the tourist brochures.

The reason for emphasizing this European dilemma here is that it is so much like the situation in Asia: in both areas, local ethnic groups either were successful in resisting efforts to be absorbed or were absorbed with a consequent loss of identity. Asia has traditionally presented such an incredibly heterogeneous cultural face because its many cultures have managed to survive the conforming cements of the great traditions of history. In many cases, the political exponents of that tradition found it more glorious to boast of their rule over a variety of identifiable peoples than to proclaim dominance over one. There is no doubt that should the power of big governments in Eurasia slacken in the future, a thousand more nations would come into being. And most of them would have ancient sovereignties and colorful tradition to support their claim to identity.

In this context, then, traditional Asia can be divided into more than simply great and little traditions, for many Asian nations are amalgams of historical cultural entities, some of which, with their own great and little themes, still retain their identity.

The great traditions of costume in Asia are not, of course, like those of the West. A tendency prevails in Asia to observe a tradition of costume rather than to change according to "style." Richness, history, and religion are major factors in Asian elite dress. The gold and silver saris of Benares, the Tartar-style cap said to have been worn by Genghis Khan, and the green turban of those who have made the pilgrimage to Mecca are examples. Asians have always put great stock in the symbols of faith, heritage, and princely wealth; even among the sophisticated elite change according to style has been rare. This conservatism has tended to preserve aspects of traditional dress, so that even today the kimono, sari, and caftan, each ancient in origin, represent certain peoples as "national" costumes.

THE CIRCLES OF ETHNOHISTORY

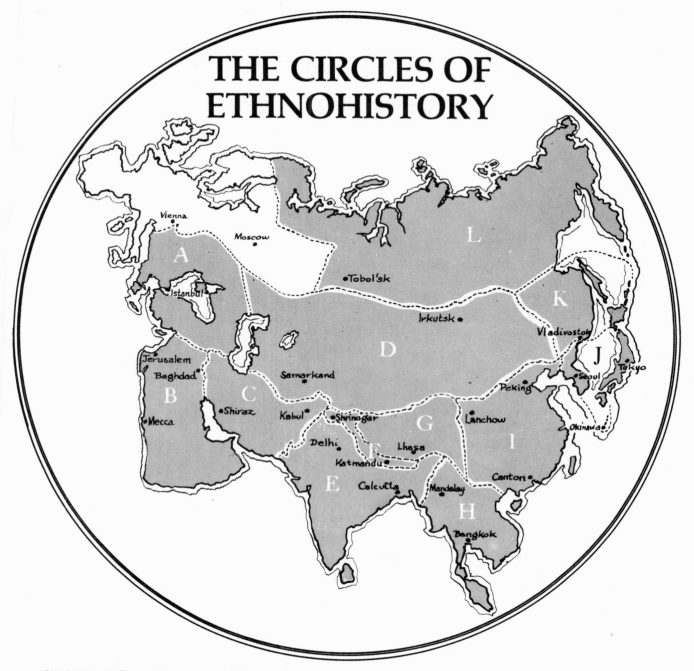

CIRCLE A: Balkans, Caucasus, and Ukraine
CIRCLE B: Near East
CIRCLE C: Iran (Persia) and Afghanistan
CIRCLE D: Central Asia
CIRCLE E: India and Pakistan
CIRCLE F: The High Borderlands
       Kashmir, Nepal, Sikkim, and Bhutan

CIRCLE G: Tibet
CIRCLE H: Southeast Asia
CIRCLE I: China
CIRCLE J: Japan and Korea
CIRCLE K: Southeast Siberia, Manchuria,
       Hokkaido, and Bonins
CIRCLE L: Siberia

III

THE CIRCLES OF ETHNOHISTORY

Quite apart from civilized centers and their widespread influence, there are clearly defined cultural zones within Eurasia. Excluding the block of Europeans, Scandinavians, and industrialized Russians who are exponents of Western civilization, it is possible to define twelve zones, or "circles," whose historical and cultural backgrounds make them distinct from one another. This concept, which was originally set forth by Elizabeth Bacon, has been applied to the costumes presented in this book and is illustrated by the map shown on the preceding page. The twelve sections that follow (Circle A through Circle L) correspond to those lettered areas on the map and describe the traditional costumes of each cultural zone.

CIRCLE A:
Balkans, Caucasus, Ukraine

This is the major contact zone where central Asians and Europeans interacted, often belligerently. Its western edge is marked by the marchland of Austria, its northern by the Russian taiga, its southern by the eastern Mediterranean, and its eastern

SOUTHERN MACEDONIA. Woman's costume — style worn before World War II. Wool vest and apron; cotton tunic, bib, and underdress, all decorated with wool and cotton embroidery, sequins, lace, and pearl beads. Coins from Turkey, Bulgaria, and Yugoslavia dangle from silver chains. At the back, a false braid ornament, made of black silk, hangs from the shoulders.

MACEDONIA (Skoplje region). Woman's costume, nineteenth and early twentieth centuries, worn on Sundays and festive occasions. Made of linen, wool, and felt, heavily embroidered and decorated with braids, laces, ribbons, metallic threads, sequins, and pearl-like beads.
A detail is shown above.

GEORGIA (Caucasus region).
Man's costume, nineteenth and
early twentieth centuries. Wool
coat with bullet pouches, wool
trousers, silk shirt, wool hat with
karakul fur trim.

TURKEY (Aydin). Woman's costume, nineteenth and early twentieth centuries, worn in the home. When outside, women covered themselves with a cloak and face veil. Satin, brocaded with metallic silver, floral pattern.

CENTRAL SERBIA (Sumadija).
Woman's costume, nineteenth and
early twentieth centuries. Wool
apron, socks, and accordion-
pleated skirt; cotton blouse
decorated with embroidery and
lace; jacket of sheepskin.

SOUTHERN MACEDONIA ▶
(Skocivir village). Man's costume,
nineteenth and early twentieth
centuries. Wool jacket and vest
trimmed with braid, cotton tunic,
beaded bib.

46

47

GREECE (Delphi). Woman's costume. Felt jacket
heavily encrusted with metallic silver embroidery,
sequins, and silver braid. These jackets are
worked by tailors whose only trade is this type of
embroidery. Called "graphta," it is done
over a traced design.

by the Caspian Sea. At its heart is Istanbul, known as Constantinople until 1930 and by the ancient world as Byzantium. All but its northern reaches — the steppes of the Ukraine and the Hungarian plain — are mountainous. Except for India, it is the seat of more diversity of peoples than anywhere in Eurasia. The cultural foundation of the region derives from the ancient Greeks, whose trading enterprise carried Greek culture to the mouths of the great Eurasian rivers: the Danube, the Dniester, the Volga, and the Don. In turn, Romans, Byzantines, and Ottoman Turks succeeded in maintaining the links between the Aegean, Anatolian, Balkan, and Ukrainian realms.

Ethnically the region is dissimilar almost from valley to valley. Muslim Albanians are found far to the west, while Christian Armenians battle for survival in the Caucasian hills. The Aegean Greeks, the Anatolian Turks, and the Magyars of Hungary may claim ethnic purity, but the bulk of the region's population is a mixture of peoples who have been integrated there over the centuries. Some, like the Kurds on the south and the Cossacks on the north, have a hybrid origin; they emerged as an amalgam out of the exiles, refugees, and the disenfranchised who found a common theme. The region in this regard is both a bridge across which trade, armies, and migrating peoples have moved, and a refuge where minority peoples could survive the annihilating forces of history.

The region is generally cool in climate, though the Mediterranean shores are warm. Wool is the most common clothing fabric, but goat hair and leather are also used extensively. Silk, cotton, and linen are worn mostly for formal dress. The economy is predominantly agricultural, giving emphasis to village life, from which much of the variety within the costume of a given region derives.

The Turks are the most numerous people in the region, and their influence was very great until 1918. The Turkish pantaloon (chalwar), the blouse or chemise (entari), and the caftan coat are thus widely used by women in the southern part of the region from the Balkans to the Caucasus. The veil (yashmak), once common among the Muslims of the region, was generally abandoned after the revolution of 1918.

Men wore variations of the pantaloon-blouse combination with a waistcoat and outer cloak. The fez, once the traditional mark of the Muslim, disappeared with Mustafa Kemal, the president of Turkey from 1923 to 1938.

In their traditional dress, the Greeks exhibit both Turkish influence and their indigenous ancestry. The latter is best exemplified by the clothing of the evzone, or select infantryman, of the army who wears pleated kilts (fustanella), a bolero, and a Phrygian cap. Typical, however, of much of traditional Greek dress for men is the Turkish-style pantaloon. Women wear tunics over blouses and skirts and often vests in much of Greece and the Balkans, while scarves and handkerchiefs are typical head coverings.

EXAMPLES OF COSTUME VARIATION WITHIN CIRCLE A:

1. Greek man
2. 19th-century Turkish man
3. Greek woman
4. 19th-century Turkish man
5. Herzegovinian man
6. Traditional Turko-Caucasian sword
7. Herzegovinian woman

8. Ukrainian woman
9. Turko-Caucasian boots
10. Cossack man
11. Cossack woman
12. Russian woman
13. Ukrainian-Caucasian man
14. Hungarian man

The rich embroidery with which all these costumes are embellished gives them color and beauty. Distinguishing costume characteristics in subregions of large areas of the Balkans are often apparent only in the nature of the embroidered decoration or background color.

The Caucasus was strongly influenced by the Turks, and so the *tarboosh* (a hat similar to the fez), the caftan, the veil, and the pantaloon are found there even among the Armenians. However, the Georgians, more successful in their resistance to Turkish rule, reflect the influence of the Ukraine, even though the pantaloon is popular among them.

A favorite of this mountain region, and indeed characteristic of it, is the male's bullet-pouched overdress. Worn short or long, it is found among the Georgians, and on the plains, among the Cossacks. A sash or belt to which is tied a straight short sword, boots over the legs of rather baggy trousers, and a wide-sleeved blouse complete the outfit. This clothing is ideally suited for horsemen since it provides looseness for riding, as well as protection against the climate. Women in the Ukraine frequently wear a long skirt-blouse with full sleeves. The skirt is covered by a wraparound and/or apron tied at the waist. A sleeveless coat that hangs just below the waist and overlaps in front gives an Oriental appearance; this is not strange, considering the central Asian influences in the region. Embroidery at wrist, throat, and upper arms and bold patterns on the aprons and overskirts make these costumes very colorful. Flowered headpieces with gay, long ribbons attached are typical in the Ukraine and parts of the Caucasus. Boots are worn by women as well as men.

Distinctive fur headgear, usually made of karakul sheepskin, is worn by men from the Caucasus to the Carpathians. The Cossacks prefer a raked style, while the Caucasians vary from the huge domes of the Muslim Turks to the rather modest cylinders of the Georgians.

Proceeding westward across the open lands from the Ukraine to Vienna, one finds variations on these styles. Hungarians, Transylvanians, and Romanians put much emphasis on cloaks, capes, short sleeveless jackets, broad-brimmed hats, and tight-fitting pants. Long and short tunics are also frequently seen. Women continue the tradition of full-sleeved blouses, aprons, and long underskirts. The amount of embroidery and rich color used in these costumes for both men and women is extraordinary. It has been said that there are none more splendid among the costumes of the world than the ordinary traditional dress of the people of these lands and the neighboring Balkans. Certainly this can well be believed.

The tight-fitting pants and broad-brimmed hats of the men and the embroidered tight-fitting bodices of western Hungarian women indicate the western end of a Eurasian circle and the beginning of the truly European world that takes us, appropriately, to the gates of Vienna.

Today most of these costumes are relics. Eastern Europe is largely communized; the Ukraine, Turkey, and the Caucasus are Russianized (which means Westernized). Only in parts of Greece, Yugoslavia, and Romania does some of the older traditional dress survive as a part of the daily life of the people. The aesthetic loss to the world of the unembarrassed, full-fledged, and prideful use of these splendid costume traditions is a great one, but what that loss means locally in terms of self-identity, security, and progress is incalculable.

CIRCLE B:
Near East

The region is made up of a largely Semitic-speaking people who inhabit an area stretching from Syria, south to Suez, and eastward to include the valley of the Tigris-Euphrates and the vast Arabian desert plateau. This circle contains the historic Fertile Crescent, seat of ancient civilizations and the homeland of biblical fame. Since this land intervenes between the Iranian plateau, central Asia, and the Mediterranean lands on the one hand and the sea roads of the Red Sea, the Arabian Sea, and the Persian Gulf on the other, the area has always had great strategic importance for both mercantile generals and empire builders. Traditionally called the Near East, it was recently renamed the Middle East, dividing Asia into Middle East, Far East, and Southeast Asia, but at the same time leaving major segments undesignated. In order to avoid confusion, in this book the traditional usage of Near East — in terms of culture, history, and modern scholarship — has been retained.

The traditions of the older Near East are strongly reflected in the traditions there today. Anyone who has read biblical literature will be immediately aware of one salient feature of the Near East — that a great many peoples have entered the region for one reason or another. All have left their mark, but those who stayed became Near Eastern, emulating for the most part the lives and customs of those who had been there before. As early as 2000 B.C., "Asiatics" were known to the Egyptians. The bearded and draped men they depicted are not unlike some seen in Damascus in more recent times — in fact, the beard is still worn by older men as a mark of male dignity. From ancient times, wherever good graphic descriptions are preserved in monument or text, there are aspects of modern traditional costumes. Evidence for the *barracan,* for example, a piece of cloth six feet or more in length wrapped sari-like about the body and pulled over a woman's shoulders and head, and the *khalak,* a headpiece or veil, with its back length falling below the waist, reaches back at least to the Roman conquest, and this clothing was most likely centuries old by then.

LEBANON. Traditional sheik's costume still worn today, except in city, for everyday wear. In cold weather, a black cloak *(aba)* goes over the costume. The type of fez shown is worn after the pilgrimage to Mecca. The jacket is made of four loom pieces, warp striped; the inner coat *(gimbaz)* is of wool worsted with braid trim.

In contrast to the diversity of Circle A, this circle has some uniformity of costume. There are two primary reasons for this. First, Islam is the faith of almost all the peoples of the Near East, the important and major exception being the people of the state of Israel. (Israel, however, is a modern state and its people are largely devotees of Western dress.) The second reason is concerned with geographical setting. Most of the land of the Near East is barren desert, often mountainous, but more frequently wide open, waterless, and sandy. Whether blowing hot or cold, winds are strong and bitter. This is the land of the Bedouin wanderers, who move seasonally wherever grass and water are found. There are many groups among the Bedouin, for their unities are local and patriarchal. Rich in tradition and daredevil in spirit, they owe ultimate allegiance to themselves only. When the final annihilation of older cultures occurs in the apocalypse of modernization, the Bedouin undeniably will be the last champion of the old ways.

The eastern Mediterranean coastal region (the so-called Levant), the inner valleys where some rainfall from the sea annually waters alluvial soils, the larger oases, and the great riverine systems of the Tigris-Euphrates are the basis for the second way of Near Eastern life — that of the sedentary world. Here arose the folk order of the farming villages and the great traditions of such famed mercantile cities as Baghdad, Damascus, Beirut, and Mosul, and the holy cities of Mecca and Jerusalem.

EXAMPLES OF COSTUME VARIATION WITHIN CIRCLE B:

1. Iraqi girl
2. Yemenite elder
3. Sinai desert woman
4. Arabian man
5. Iraqi boy
6. Palestinian village woman
7. Saudi Arabian woman

8. Syrian dervish
9. Syrian dervish
10. Traditional Arab from Syria and Arabia
11. Saudi Arabian man
12. Bedouin woman
13. Yemenite boy
14. Bedouin woman

54

The Bedouin male costume is not unlike that of the sedentary Arab in much of the Near East. Usually a cotton shirt *(kamis* or *galabia)* that reaches almost to the ground is tied at the waist with a sash or belt. The *aba,* a sleeveless coat made of animal hair or coarse cotton, usually dark in color and often edged in black, silver, or gold, has a cape-like quality among the Bedouin. Vests or short coats are often worn under the aba. Sandals and shoes are worn by men, even by horsemen. The Bedouin man wears the typical headdress of the Near Eastern Arab. It consists of the *kaffiyeh,* or headcloth, held on the head and given substance by a double band of cord, called the *agal.* The agal can be decorated in a number of ways; frequently gold or silver thread, pompons, or special knots are added. The kaffiyeh of the Bedouin, and of Arabs in general, may be made of rough cotton or the finest silk.

The long-sleeved caftan robe, usually of cotton, overlaps in front and is often held in place with a sash or belt. This is worn under the aba when the two are combined.

Women generally wear variations of the veil, since traditionally purdah (the

SYRIA (Jebel Druze). Traditional costume still worn today by young Druze men. Jacket is of wool, as are the braid-trimmed trousers that, typically, have many pleats at the crotch.

seclusion of women from public view) is observed. This covering varies from long, body-concealing robes to simple face masks. Head coverings, either as separate pieces of cloth or as a part of the long and flowing *gandoura,* which often reaches the ground, are common elements of women's clothing. Robes or dresses that reach to the ankle or longer are worn loosely, presumably for ease of motion and air circulation.

The Arab woman loves jewelry and wears as much of it as possible. Necklaces, earrings, hair pieces, rings, anklets, and above all bracelets are worn in great profusion, especially among the Bedouin. A veiled woman marks her way by the tinkle and clank of her ornaments, unseen but certainly heard.

Embroidery, stamped and woven in floral and geometric designs, is commonplace in the decoration of women's inner clothing but infrequent on the outer clothing except on formal occasions. The exception appears to be found among the sedentary peoples of the Levant. Here Christians, Muslims, and Jews at one time vied with one another in the decoration and style of women's clothing. Now, community after community has its particular costume variation, so that one can speak of a Bethlehem style, a Jerusalem style, or a Damascus style and refer to precisely recognizable costumes. Generally these costumes also differ in color and place of embroidery, and the headdresses are exceptionally dramatic. They include the tarboosh with veil *(yashmak),* a tall conical or cylindrical hat sometimes called the *shatweh,* and a variety of high and low headdresses decorated with gold or silver coins.

As mentioned previously, the modern state of Israel has not evolved a characteristic national costume, having accepted Western modes almost entirely. The exceptions are, of course, the various kinds of rabbinical garb and the rapidly vanishing costumes of immigrant Jews from countries such as Yemen that still hold to their own form of costumes.

SYRIA (Jebel Druze). Druze bride's costume,
worn today, shows Western influence. Damascus
brocade dress, with nylon crepe and tulle for
apron, scarf, and ruffles. Gold-colored metal
filigree ornament at waist represents fish and
moons; hat has silver filigree disk and
gold-colored metal "coins."

SYRIA (village of Amouq Valley).
Man's costume, nineteenth
century. Wool vest and trousers,
cotton shirt, hand-spun and
hand-woven. Felt fez.

PALESTINE (Bethlehem). Arab woman's costume, nineteenth century to the present, worn for festive occasions. Cotton and silk gown, velvet jacket; both pieces embroidered with metallic and silk threads appliquéd to fabric. Embroidered cap decorated with gold-colored "coins" and red stone beads. This costume is about fifty years old.

ARABIAN PENINSULA. Traditional man's costume, still worn today by men from almost all walks of life in all the countries of the Arabian Peninsula. This wool cloak with gilt braid (aba) is for winter wear and is often black. In other seasons, the cloak is lighter in weight and may be light tan or off-white. The cotton headcloth, white or checked in red or black, is worn wrapped around the face in the desert. The type of head cord shown is worn by the royal family of Saudi Arabia and its guards; others wear a narrow black cord.

IRAQ. Man's costume, belonged ▶ to Prince Said of Iraq before 1919. Said was the youngest son of King Husein of Hejaz, first of the Hashimite kings. Satin brocaded with metallic gold.

60

SYRIA (village of Amouq Valley). Woman's
costume, nineteenth century; worn today for
festive occasions. Silk and cotton gown with
hand-embroidered panels, cap and chain
decorated with silver- and gold-colored metal
"coins." A detail is shown at right.

62

BALUCHISTAN (West Pakistan and southeastern
Iran). Traditional girl's costume for everyday
use is still worn today. Silk dress and trousers
have typical Baluch-style embroidered panels,
whose patterns vary among the Baluch tribes.

EASTERN AFGHANISTAN
(Pathan). Traditional shepherd's
costume *(pushtin)*, still worn today.
Sheepskin coat and vest with
silk embroidery.

CENTRAL AFGHANISTAN
(Hazara). Man's costume,
nineteenth century. Camel hair
coat with silk, wool, and metallic
embroidery and appliqué work;
cap of sheepskin.

IRAN. Man's costume, nineteenth
century to the present. Traditional
everyday dress of farmers and
peasants. Camel hair coat with
appliquéd cotton embroidery,
braid edging of Paisley
twill weave.

IRAN (Teheran). Woman's
costume; modern version of a
traditional style. Silk and metallic
gold brocade coat, satin gown
with sequin decoration.

AFGHANISTAN. Hats *(kolas)* of
the Tajik, Pathan, Uzbek, and
Turkmen peoples (primarily
northern Afghanistan).

CIRCLE C:
Iran (Persia) and Afghanistan

No country in Asia can rival Iran, the ancient Persia, in its list of major contributors to the world's humanistic order. Gifted poets, philosophers, narrators, observers, gardeners, architects, and many artists were born, raised, and inspired in this vast bridgeland of inner western Asia. Some such as Zoroaster, Omar Khayyám, Hafiz, Saadi, Firdausi, and Rashid gained world renown, and their fame emphasizes the rich, motivating cultural environment from which they sprang. From those most ancient days when the Elamites competed with the Sumerians for cultural ascendancy at the dawn of civilization, through the rise of Achaemenid Persia as the greatest imperium of ancient times, to the vibrant Partho-Sassanian world that lay frustratingly just beyond the bounds of Roman imperial ambition, Iran combined cultural influences from many parts of Eurasia into a unique whole. Even the recalcitrant Greeks, who saw Persia as realistically as a warring people could, admitted to a sense of awe when confronted with the splendors of the House of Cyrus and Darius. The history of Iran's culture can be described not only as innovative but, paradoxically, also as rich in tradition. Thus the coming of Islam in the eighth century A.D. with its iconoclastic conversion of the people to the new faith was not as drastic as it was for other cultures of the Near East. Iran adopted Shi'a Islam and gave it native form, the iconoclasm was diluted, and what emerged were the splendors of miniature painting and the delicacy of figured ceramics. Even the architecture reflected elements of the old Iranian culture. In this way Islamic Iran became a new achievement, one that to this day has maintained a certain momentum. The world might well look to Iran to see how its culture will react to the conquests of Western industrialization. Will cheap machine-made goods and conditioned human minds bring Iran's unique cultural achievements to a close? Or will Iran rise again — in a new achievement equal to those of her past?

Afghanistan, on the eastern end of the Iranian plateau, is a comparatively recent kingdom that arose out of the empire of Nadir Shah in the eighteenth century. However, it has a long history that marks its essential sovereignty from at least the days when it broke away from the empire set up by Seleucus, one of Alexander's generals, and as the Kingdom of Bactriana dominated the region for several centuries. As with Iran, Afghanistan has been subject to many influences, particularly from India and central Asia. This is, of course, in keeping with its strategic position across main routes between east and west, north and south.

Both Afghanistan and Iran count many different ethnic groups within their

EXAMPLES OF COSTUME VARIATION WITHIN CIRCLE C:

1. Afghan man from Kabul
2. Afghan woman from Kabul
3. Baluch man from southern Afghanistan
4. Pathan woman from Afghanistan
5. Uzbek man from northern Afghanistan
6. Pathan man from Afghanistan

7. Pushtin jacket from Afghanistan
8. Mullah from Herat-Meshed area
9. Traditional Iranian woman
10. Iranian woman from Caspian region
11. Central Iranian man
12. Kashgai man from western Iran
13. Traditional Iranian turban

borders. The Afghans, for example, include the Pathans, the largest group, and sizable representations of Tajik, Uzbek, Hazara, Turkmen, Kirghiz, and Baluch. The basic population of Iran is sedentary and includes the Tajik and other Iranian people. However, there are seminomadic groups such as the Baktiari, Kashgai, and the Lurs in the west, and Baluch in the southeast. Arabs are found in the southwest, Armenians and Azerbaijani in the northwest, and Turkmen in the northeast. These groups should be considered in discussing the costumes of Iran, but they are better described in the circle in which they have larger representation.

The basic traditional costume for men in Iran consists of trousers, a long shirt held with a sash, a sleeved cloak, and a small, rather stiff hat *(kola)*, the latter made of cloth, felt, or lambskin. The kola has wider variation as one moves eastward, until in Afghanistan and western Turkestan it is found in many colorfully decorated styles in which embroidery and sequins have a prominent place. Afghan men wear pantaloons *(tombon)* loosely around the legs. Tunics or long shirts are worn outside the pantaloon. These are sometimes pleated; in fact, pleating is a characteristic costume feature for both men and women, particularly on formal occasions. The most colorful elements of men's garb are the vest and waistcoat. Here the tailor really excels in applying gold, silver, or colored embroidery to the richest cloth obtainable. A silk or velvet background for beautiful traditional designs in embroidery is commonly seen in Kabul, and even a poor man may have a colorful vest of dyed sheepskin or felt. Tiny mirrors sewn onto these Afghan waistcoats and vests mark the approximate western limits of this decorative technique.

Turbans are a common sight in Afghanistan, but they were banned with the modernization of Iran. The turban of Iran still occurs among religious figures, however — the last vestige of a colorful and meaningful tradition. Most turbans are worn rather informally in Afghanistan and among the tribesmen of the adjacent northwest territories of West Pakistan. Usually a longish piece of cloth (six yards plus) is simply wrapped about the head with one end left loose for a face cloth. However, on more formal occasions or because of the wearer's occupation or status, a kola is worn as a core about which the turban is carefully wound. The folding in front is given special attention, as it not only enhances the appearance of the individual but traditionally the forehead is exposed for prayer purposes. Starching the end of the cloth to make it stand upright from its tuck in the top of the turban is a custom among the military in West Pakistan.

The great cloak *(pushtin)* is made of sheepskin with the wool on the inside for warmth in winter. It has sleeves, but these are usually left flapping while the individual exposes only his head from the ample depth of this efficient and often colorfully decorated covering.

Both Iranian and Afghan women have observed purdah. The Afghans even

AFGHANISTAN (Kabul). Purdah (concealment of women) costume, traditionally worn in public. The silk veil is hand-embroidered.

today still adhere to the custom. One often sees these women completely enveloped in the *chadan*, a voluminous cloak that hangs from head to feet and is open in front, or in a *burka*, a pleated robe with attached headpiece that tightly covers the entire head. Pantaloons, embroidered vests, and a variety of kolas are traditionally worn by Afghan women. In Iran, dresses are commonplace, and they are rapidly gaining popularity among the city women of Afghanistan.

The Afghans still retain the pointed shoes of the past. The most exotic are those with upturned toes, of which considerable variety are worn by women and men alike.

CIRCLE D:
Central Asia

Central Asia is the kingdom of the horse nomad. This explains why this particular circle covers such a vast part of Asia, extending from eastern Manchuria to the boundaries of the Ukraine. Within this zone stand such famed cities as Samarkand, Bukhara, and Tashkent. Lying across trade routes between east and west, these centers became rich seats of power and nomadic groups warred over their control. Not all central Asians were nomadic, however. A considerable number provided sedentary support for the khanates (regions ruled by the khans, or local chieftains) of western central Asia as well as for the craftsmen who gave the cities their world fame. Thus, when speaking of central Asia one refers to two basically different ways of life: the sedentary and the pastoral nomadic.

The sedentary population of western central Asia traditionally dressed in the Persian mode – trousers, shirt, sleeved cloak (dolman), and kola or turban. The traditional clothing of the pastoral nomad, however, received influences from past conquests and occupation, as well as from direct contemporary contact. Central Asia is the region where such processes as quilting, felting, and rug weaving originated and developed. The nomadic populations make most of their textiles from wool and hair, but cotton is most frequently used by the sedentary. Today, for example, Uzbekistan is the largest cotton-producing region of the Soviet Union. Silk, always prized by central Asians, gave the wearer of silken garments a certain prestige in the heyday of the khanates.

Most central Asians of both sexes wear boots of felt or leather, with pant legs tucked in. A blouse or other undergarment for the upper part of the body is put on, and then the whole is covered over with a belted or girdled outer garment. In western central Asia (Uzbekistan, Tadzhikistan, Kazakstan, Turkmenistan, and Kirgizia) the caftan or the dolman is used as the outer garment. The tunic with its higher hem occurs among the more nomadic people. In eastern central Asia (Mongolian territories, eastern Manchuria, and among the Buryat and southern Yakut of Siberia) the del is commonly the outer garment. This is a robe pulled across the body to make a double layer in front in the Chinese fashion. In winter all these people, east and west, wear heavy robes of fur or hair, usually cut in the style of the caftan, dolman, or del, depending on the customs of the particular ethnic group.

Central Asians enjoy color in their costume, and whether using an ikat (yarns are tied and dyed before weaving) or an embroidery or a print the colors tend to be

EXAMPLES OF COSTUME VARIATION WITHIN CIRCLE D:

1. Turkmen man
2. Turkmen woman
3. Kazakh man
4. Kazakh woman
5. Uzbek man

6. Kazakh chief
7. through 10. Mongol headdresses
11. Mongol woman
12. Mongol woman
13. Mongol man

prime and rich. Deep reds, blues, and greens are often background colors of robes, against which jewelry, handsome belts, velvet jackets, or fine sashes stand out.

Hats and headdresses are the most divergent and striking elements in central Asian costume. In the nineteenth century an ethnic group could be identified on the basis of hats alone: the large sheep's wool or lambskin hats of the Turkmen; the gaily colored Uzbek *tyubeterka* (similar to a kola); the cup hat with central peak of the Mongols and the elaborate headdresses of the Mongol women; and the so-called Tartar hat — a round pyramidal hat surrounded by a brim of fur.

TURKMENISTAN and NORTH AFGHANISTAN (Turkmen). Traditional man's costume with karakul fur hat. The quilted cotton jacket is also worn by the horsemen who play Buzkashi, a game similar to polo.

Because central Asian nomad women did a man's work in their daily routine, their costume, except for the headdress, differed very little from that of men. Even Muslim nomads in this region did not seclude their women. On formal occasions such as weddings, finely worked costumes were worn by women as well as by men. These were usually elaborations on traditional clothing in which the amount of ornamentation and jewelry might give prestige to the wearer or his family.

Warmth, ease of movement, and personal prestige, then, seem to have been the major governing factors in the development of central Asian costume.

How to tie a conventional turban.

BUKHARA (Soviet Republic of Turkmenistan).
Woman's costume, nineteenth century. Dress with
house shoes. The cloak and cap were worn in
the street with a face veil and often with boots
to the knee. The dress of silk with metallic brocade,
decorated at the waist with silvery metal and
yarn pendants, is about sixty years old. It was
the property of the late Emir of Bukhara. Ikat
woven silk cape.

Circle D

77

TURKMENISTAN and NORTH AFGHANISTAN
(Turkmen). Traditional woman's costume worn
today by women who work on rug-making looms.
Large amounts of heavy jewelry and head
ornaments are worn at all times. Silk dress
(kurta) is hand-embroidered and silk trousers are
decorated with sequins. Scarf is block-printed.

SIBERIA (Yakut). Woman's costume,
nineteenth century, winter wear. Various Arctic
furs, wool flannel, silk and gilt brocade and
embroidery. Hanging from silver chains at the
waist are pouches, pendants, chains with
crosses, tweezers, etc.

SIBERIA (Yakut). Shaman's costume. Cowskin
with metal attachments of bells and clackers,
which rattle as shaman dances and beats a drum.
Disks and long thin pendants represent bones
and internal organs. The coat weighs about
thirty pounds.

MONGOLIA. Monk's costume. The coat was a present from the Abbot of the Gandon Monastery in Ulan Bator to a visiting Buddhist monk from Nepal. Silk damask with velvet and cotton trim, sheepskin lining.

INDIA (Maharashtra state, Aurangabar village). Sari of silk, ends brocaded with gold thread.

Circle E

INDIA. Paisley samples, silk and wool twill weave.

81

INDIA (Kutch region, Rabari tribe). Traditional man's, woman's, and child's costumes, used at present time for everyday wear. The Rabaris are pastoral nomads. Cotton with hand embroidery and mirror work.

INDIA (Hyderabad, Banjara tribe). Traditional woman's costume, still worn today. European gypsy costumes resemble those of the Banjaras. Silver earrings, arm and ankle bracelets, finger and toe rings are worn with this costume. Garments are cotton with mirror work and embroidery. ▶

83

WEST PAKISTAN (Sind).
Traditional woman's costume.
Silk and cotton with mirror work
and embroidery.

CIRCLE E:
India and Pakistan

The late B. Subbarao, an Indian scholar of great perception, divided the Indian subcontinent into three zones defined by their ethnic and historical roles. The first of his zones was called the "Zone of Attraction." This consists basically of the great Indus and Ganges-Jumna river valley systems of northern India-Pakistan. Located along these rivers are such heavily populated and world-renowned regions as the Punjab and Bengal and a roster of exotic cities that includes Lahore, Peshawar, Delhi, Lucknow, Benares, and Calcutta. The second zone is labeled the "Zone of Relative Attraction" and is made up of regions that border the first zone but include much of peninsular India and the now heavily populated coasts. The third zone is the "Zone of Isolation" – the homeland of India's primitive tribes and nomadic pastoralists – characterized by deserts, rain forests, and mountain areas remote from the center of attraction.

This zoning scheme for the Indo-Pakistan subcontinent is of considerable value to the student of costume, for it helps to explain the presence of certain styles and fashions in any given region. The Zone of Attraction gains its character from foreign invaders who came through the Khyber and other western passes and usually settled in this zone. Here were established their cities, the centers of imperial control — until the next invader! Because of this historical phenomenon, considerable change appeared in the costume of the elite who ruled the lands of northern India. This is noticeable in the coinage, figurines, statues, and other graphic material that are part of the archeological record of the north. While the Mogul period, which lasted from about the time of Columbus's discovery of America to the Indian mutiny in 1857, was marked by artistic splendor fully comparable in its way to the Italian Renaissance, it paradoxically failed to create a unique costume style. Instead, Persian costume was adopted, even by some of the Hindu rajas who were vassals of the Moguls. Thus, the richly woven long coats, pants, and colorful turbans of Islamic Persia, along with the pointed shoes of that tradition, can be seen as the main costume in countless miniature paintings depicting the aristocracy at home, at court, and in the field. This has remained the typical style in the Punjab and in West Pakistan. As the *shalwa-kamis* it is now the national costume for Pakistani women, who wear it without the coat. Instead, a scarf *(dupatta)* is used as head covering or shoulder drape.

Today's urbanized men in both northern India and Pakistan wear loose-fitting trousers and a shirt left outside the trousers, both usually white. These men frequently go without head covering, but the lamb's wool kola and the Gandhi cloth cap are commonly seen; the former in West Pakistan and the latter, of course, in India.

Village India in both the Zones of Attraction and Relative Attraction has as its characteristic dress the dhoti for men and the sari for women. The dhoti is simply a cloth wraparound that can be worn shirt length or tied between the legs as a loincloth to free the lower limbs. Village men frequently go bare from the waist up, but sometimes wear loose-fitting short-sleeved shirts. Village people everywhere typically wear no shoes.

It has been said with reason that the sari is the most feminine costume in the world. Its origins are obscure. One theory has it derived from the Roman toga, which it resembles, and another would have its beginnings in the draped robes of the Holy Land, which may date from as early as 1000 B. C. These theories, however, remain theories. What is abundantly clear is that the sari is a graceful response to the exigencies of India's hot climate. The sari costume consists of three essential parts: the *choli* piece, which covers the upper part of the body but leaves the midriff bare; the skirt or petticoat, held to the body by a drawstring; and the sari piece, the long (six to ten yards), often decorated cloth of silk for the wealthy, or of simple cotton for ordinary use. One end of the sari is tucked into the petticoat at the waist, wound completely about the hips, and then carried over one shoulder. The remaining end can be used as a head or face covering. The most common method of draping a sari is illustrated on page 89. In the past, local tastes tended to regionalize the color and the kind of decoration used on the sari, but this is increasingly obscured by mass production of sari cloth. Benares is still celebrated for its saris made from gold or silver thread, but because these are melted down when no longer wanted, it is rare today to find old saris from this city.

Pathan woman's and man's costumes from West Pakistan.

EXAMPLES OF COSTUME VARIATION WITHIN CIRCLE E:

1. Rajasthani man
2. Rajasthani nomad woman from Lambadi
3. Indian sari for everyday wear
4. Muslim man from northern India
5. Urban Indian man from Bombay
6. Snake charmer from Uttar Pradesh

7. Punjabi woman
8. Jaipur man
9. "Nehru" style
10. Sikh man
11. Indian sari for more
    formal wear

These general costume tendencies in the Zone of Attraction and in urbanized India should not obscure the fact that there is more variation in costume within this zone than in comparable areas of the rest of the world. For one thing, caste still has a formidable place in India's social and occupational structure. Brahmins tend toward simple overall clothing quite distinct from that of the other castes, while these, in turn, may proclaim their identity through various costume elements. Groups such as the Sikhs may wear Western clothing, but their characteristic turban marks their presence. The Jains and Parsees, who have especially adopted urban life, wear distinctive costume elements for rituals but use Western clothing on other occasions.

The Zone of Relative Attraction is where one confronts incredible variation in costume. Southern India has retained its special character since medieval times, as has Rajasthan, the largely desert region to the southwest of Delhi. Variation is less a matter of drastically different costume form than one of decoration or wearing style. The mirror work of seminomadic groups of Kutch and Rajasthan, for example, varies in design and pattern from tribe to tribe, as do the woodblock-printed designs of village costume to the east of that region. Provincial distinctions still hold in this zone, and only a little familiarity is necessary to enable one to distinguish the Orissan costume cloth on the northeast from that of Kerala on the southwest. It is this variety that marks Indian costume so graphically and makes the subcontinent one of the most colorful costume regions of the earth.

The primitive groups of the Zone of Isolation have characteristic costumes, and their variety adds its massive contribution to the costume eminence that is India's today. The tribal costume for daily purposes is generally a simple garment, but for ritual or formal occasions it can be very elaborate. The Naga of Assam, for example, have costumes that consist of a dozen or more separate pieces. Since the government of India lists over 400 scheduled tribes (not all in the Zone of Isolation, however), and each of these has its own ethnocentrism often expressed in costume, the subject is a complex and fascinating one.

Since remote antiquity India has been the place where the foreigner went seeking dyes and fine cloth. A Roman seaport of the first century A. D. has been found near Pondicherry complete with dyeing vats; Daibul, the partly legendary city of the *Arabian Nights,* was a port on the west coast of India where fabulous cloth could be obtained. Today a visit to the cloth bazaar in the Chandni Chauk gives one a sense of India's ancient lure. The incredible color and fineness of weave that assault the eyes as swath after swath of streaming cloth is tossed before one create an indescribable feeling. India's dilemma is how to modernize without killing the traditions that give it identity. What happens to India's costume will mark the success or failure of answers to that dilemma.

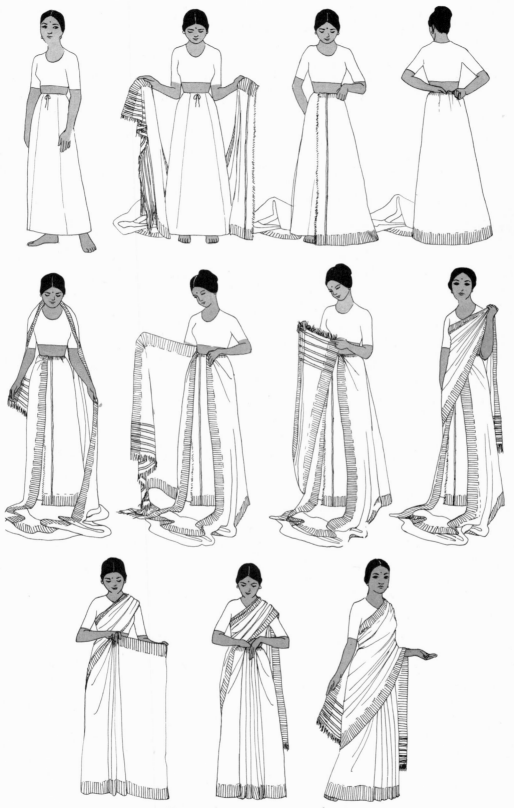

How to drape a conventional sari.

CIRCLE F:
The High Borderlands
Kashmir, Nepal, Sikkim, and Bhutan

The northern borderlands of the Indian subcontinent form a unique and colorful entity among the various regions of Asia. The country is mountainous — in fact the Karakoram-Himalaya chain includes the highest mountains on earth. Except for large fertile tracts in Kashmir and Nepal, the settled parts of the region are made up of small valleys and treed slopes where, by combining barley cultivation, truck gardening, and limited pastoralism, small, distinct peasant communities make a living. On the higher slopes and plateaus subsistence activity is largely the pastoralism of goats, sheep, and yaks with limited hunting. Trade is important and while there are no cities in this zone, there are a number of towns whose importance varies with the fortunes of commerce. Through much of the region Tibetan Buddhism flourishes, its monasteries and temples found even in the remotest reaches. Sikkim and Bhutan are Buddhist states. Nepal is Hindu, although many Buddhists live within its borders, the most famous of whom are probably the Sherpas, mountain climbers par excellence. In the west, Kashmir's people are largely Mohammedan. Animistic belief runs widely through all these areas, some institutionalized, some surviving among inhabitants like the Lepchas — whose aboriginal ancestors were the basic population in Sikkim and probably Bhutan — and the Shembas of northern Nepal.

The sari is common in Kashmir and Nepal, and forms of the dhoti are popular among the sedentary populations of the Vale proper and the valley of Katmandu. Cotton cloth is common, as is silk among the wealthy. But goat hair and sheep and yak wool are most frequently woven in the region. Tibetan-style clothing dominates in Bhutan, Sikkim, much of Nepal, and Ladakh. Differences among the costumes of these lands are apparent largely in ornamentation and local decoration styles, though hats also vary considerably. The color of a shawl and the way it is worn can designate rank or social status. Older Chinese mandarin-style dress appears among the nobility of the smaller states and substates of the region. Chinese embroidered silk once came to the bazaars via Tibetan caravans, but this trade ceased after the loss of Tibetan sovereignty.

Probably the most typical clothing of the region for men is a long, voluminous piece of cotton or wool cloth, with sleeves, held tightly to the body by a sash. Frequently it is deliberately bagged out over the sash to provide a carrying pouch. Women wear a wraparound skirt or full robe with sleeved blouse and a jacket. A sash,

EXAMPLES OF COSTUME VARIATION WITHIN CIRCLE F:

1. Bhutan man
2. Bhutan woman
3. Sikkimese priest
4. Nepalese woman from Katmandu
5. Nepalese man from Katmandu

6. Sikkimese man
7. Lepcha man from Sikkim
8. Sikkimese woman
9. Bhutan man
10. Sherpa woman from Nepal
11. Nepalese man from Katmandu

Ladakh women's and man's (center)
costumes from Kashmir.

Tibetan-style apron, and scarf are typical additions. Women's clothing includes the
shalwa-kamis, which is often very colorful, with alternating bands of red, gray,
blue, coral, and green.

Kashmir is the homeland of old weaving traditions. The beautiful and justly
famous Kashmir shawl, made from the goat's wool of the region, illustrates the high
quality of traditional weavers. Kashmiri costume, however, has been rather plain
except on formal occasions. The men's wear is similar to that of Muslim areas in
Pakistan and Afghanistan to the west — a combination of trousers (loose-fitting),
long shirt (worn outside the pants), and a vest or jacket — nowadays the latter is
Western style. The Kashmiri hat, however, is distinctive. It is a pie-shaped, cloth or
lamb's wool variant of the type of hat worn widely by Muslims in the mountain
regions west of the Tibetan culture area in Gilgit, Chitral, Hunza, Kafiristan,
and Swat.

Kashmiri women, celebrated for their beauty, do not observe purdah as a rule.
Their loose-fitting, large-sleeved robe, often reddish in color, is enhanced by jewelry
worn with a gypsy flare. The hat, embroidered or decoratively sewn, is round and
close-fitting, and jewelry often suspends directly from it. This hat, combined with
the characteristic hair style — combed into two braids — of Kashmiri women, recalls
central Asia (Circle D) and illustrates the hybrid quality of the Indian borderlands.

As the receiver of major influences from the west, north, and south, yet in
secure possession of an individual character, the cultural aspects of this circle are
both complex and readily recognizable. Its characteristic costume graphically shows
this paradox.

WESTERN NEPAL (Dolpo region, Baglung district). Traditional woman's costume, entirely of wool. Cloak and back apron are warp striped, sash has dyed crosses typical of western Nepal and Tibet. Headdress is made of brass plates fitted to wooden dowels and stitched to padded flannel. Women's hair is done into many small braids, some of which are drawn through the sides of the headdress.

KASHMIR. Woman's costume, nineteenth century,
worn by upper classes. Hat is usually covered by
a white silk scarf. Silk brocaded with metallic
gold, floral and medallion pattern. Hat is made of
gold-colored paste with red paste "jewels," seed
pearls, and metal tear-shaped pendants. A detail
is shown above.

TIBET (Lhasa). Nobleman's and noblewoman's costumes, nineteenth century. Robes and belts are silk, apron and boots wool. The woman's headdress is decorated with seed pearls and coral; her earrings and amulet box are inset with turquoise. The man's hat is fringed in silk.

Circle G

TIBET. Man's costume, traditionally worn by nomads, is entirely of wool with tie-dyed crosses on hat, sash, and coat. The usual color for these coats is maroon.

TIBET. Dancing costume, worn by monks for the "black hat wizard's" dance. This is an oracular dance connected with the Tibetan New Year. Coat, apron, and collar are of various silks and brocades. Silks, imported from China, have such Chinese motifs as dragons, clouds, and water.

100

CIRCLE G:
Tibet

Tibet lies at the center of the mountain heart of Asia. It had been the world's largest surviving theocracy until the Red Chinese took over completely in 1959. The land consists of a high barren plateau intersected by river valleys and surrounded by mountains. Sparsely inhabited, the area has its largest population in the south, where the river Tsangpo (in India it becomes the Brahmaputra) and its tributaries have created fertile valleys suitable for agriculture. Here the capital city, Lhasa, was the seat of a succession of Dalai Lamas, incarnations of the patron deity of Tibet, Avalokiteshvara. This deity, a Buddhist bodhisattva, is benign and in a very real sense provides one clue to why the feudal system, which dominated Tibetan life, was of such longevity in that immense land. Every ruler, large or small, was expected to rule in the light of the divine understanding of the bodhisattva, symbolized in the ultimate sovereign His Holiness the Dalai Lama. That the system was successful can be demonstrated best by the fierce loyalty of Tibetans to their leader and what he represents, in spite of the agonies brought to them by the modern world.

This religious orientation has preserved Tibetan traditions through time. In costume, for example, one can look at eighteenth-century paintings and see there the same costumes people were wearing in the streets of Lhasa in 1950. The priesthood, which at one time made up a sixth of the male population of Tibet, dresses simply, in keeping with the austere qualities of meditation and prayer. A wraparound robe, usually of red wool, and a cloak for cold days were traditional. However, the Tibetan Buddhist church is elaborately organized by hierarchy and by sect; the higher one's status, the richer the quality of dress. Fine silk and silk embroidery are therefore found among monks of the highest ranks. Robes and paraphernalia for ritual occasions tend to be very elaborate for most ranks. The whole wonderful panoply of masks, wands, hats, robes, flags, setting, and story brings forth a richness of color and line that delights the eye and elicits the awe so necessary to the religion. The costumes of these rituals would fill many books.

Historically, Tibet was made up of an amalgam of small, sovereign states, each of which had its own ruler. Regional traditions, therefore, derived in part from old political entities. Ethnological studies of the regional detail are lacking, and little is known of the separate cultural traditions. Yet, in women's hair styles, language dialects, and use of ornamentation and design, regional aspects are clear; these are certainly symptomatic of far deeper differences — some of which are known. The people of Ambdo in the west differ in various ways from those in Lhasa proper, as do

EXAMPLES OF COSTUME VARIATION WITHIN CIRCLE G:

1. Oracle shaman
2. Yellow-hat lama
3., 4., and 5. Tibetan male headdresses
6. Monk
7. South central Tibetan woman from Lhasa
8. Nomad woman
9. Nomad man

10. Nomad man from Kham in eastern Tibet
11. Nomad woman from Kham in eastern Tibet
12. South central Tibetan woman from Gyantse
13. Noblewoman from Lhasa
14. Man from Lhasa
15. Nobleman from Lhasa

the Kham tribesmen of the southeast from the different peoples living in the far west of Tibet proper. The study of the costume of these regions is only just beginning.

Tibetans divide secularly into the nomadic peoples who roam the plateau with their herds, descending seasonally to certain settled areas for trading purposes, and the sedentary peoples who include farming peasants and landed nobility, the latter largely urban with Lhasa as their focus. A dependent relationship exists among all these groups, since each needs the others for goods and services.

Nomads wear long loose robes of wool or hair, tightly belted with a sash or leather belt, the upper part of the robe bagging out to form a carrying pouch. Sometimes pants and usually felt or leather boots make up the rest of the costume. Fur hats, or cloth hats lined with fur, complete with ear flaps against the cold, are used by nomad and farming peasant alike.

Peasant clothes for men are either similar to those of the nomad or consist of a full robe with high collar. This robe, or *chupa,* is worn by both sexes and overlaps in front, descending to the ankles on women or priests and to the knee on men; it is bound tightly at the waist, which gives its drape a decidedly trim look. Tibetan noblemen and women also wear this costume, often making their chupas out of a particularly handsome yellow silk. The nobility, in keeping with their sedentary life, wear the robe full length. Elaborately embroidered or ornamented Chinese robes are also worn by the nobility. Tibetan noblewomen wear them on occasion, but more often the chupa is worn with an apron in front. The apron, however, seems to be more characteristic of central and eastern Tibet than of the west.

The nobility also wear a great variety of hats. The Chinese tassel or button of different colors to mark official status was adopted by Tibetan officialdom. Turquoise, coral, and pearl are particular favorites of craftsmen, and these substances are frequently found in jewelry and sewn onto hats and clothes.

Tibetan costume demonstrates, as so many other local cultural traits do, the unusual qualities of Tibetan culture. Often-heard claims that Tibetan culture is an offshoot of the Chinese or Indian cultures ignore the uniqueness that is Tibet.

EXAMPLES OF COSTUME VARIATION WITHIN CIRCLE H:

1. Vietnamese woman from Hué
2. Thai monk
3. Thai peasant
4. Meo woman from Vietnam and Laos
5. Meo man from Vietnam and Laos
6. Jarai woman from Darlac Plateau, Vietnam
7. Jarai man from Darlac Plateau, Vietnam
8. Cambodian woman

9. Cambodian man
10. Cambodian dancer
11. White Thai woman
12. Laotian woman
13. Malay woman
14. Malay man
15. Cambodian woman from Pnompenh
16. Cambodian man from Pnompenh

CIRCLE H:
Southeast Asia

The term Southeast Asia is a convenient one, for it would be difficult otherwise to find a suitable name for this vast, ethnically varied region. Politically it begins at Burma's border with India and ends at the Chinese border and the sea. However, it shares cultural features with both India and China and has had a major influence upon the islands of Indonesia. The region has been likened to a huge hand, its mountain ranges spreading north-south like great fingers, while in the valley spaces between mighty rivers flow to the sea. These rivers (Mekong, Chao Phraya, Irrawaddy, and others) rise in the high ranges of western China and Tibet and end in broad, fertile, tropical deltas on which heavy populations of rice-growing tenants reside. Rainfall is monsoonal, and forests are thick and difficult to cross. In these forests, on the high slopes of mountains, and on interior plateaus live a great number of tribal and other primitive peoples. Each group is distinct, and the result is a bewildering mosaic of ethnic entities whose study anthropologists have just begun.

The costume of these people of the hills and jungles reflects their distinct cultures. Animal and plant materials – straw, bast fiber, horn, shell, fur, hair, teeth, bone, wood, bark, and gourd – are used in varying degree depending somewhat upon the major economic emphases of the group. Cotton cloth, dyed and decorated in traditional colors, has also found an important place in the making of tribal costume. Influences from China and India, as well as from the sedentary population on the alluvial plain and valleys, have had their effect, and so wrap-arounds, pants, and shirts have found their way into tribal costume. These, however, are given traditional qualities by the use of color, jewelry, headdress, and general decoration.

Sedentary Southeast Asia has a history of many centuries, during which it developed from an animistic world into powerful Hindu, Buddhist, and Muslim kingdoms. Some, such as the Khmer and the Burmese rulers of Pagan, were master builders and creators of celebrated cities, who maintained communication with the outside world and developed a cosmopolitanism that provided a rich and hybrid foundation for the later cultural forms that were to arise.

Rice cultivation is the principal activity of the bulk of Southeast Asia's people, and so successful are they at it that their rice is exported to more needy areas of Asia. It is a life close to the earth, with family and village the main concerns of the individual. Ideologically, the people combine local superstitious belief with the high faiths of Islam or Buddhism. The latter is Hinayana Buddhism, said to be near

THAILAND (Lau Pum Dum tribe).
Bride's costume, left. Hand-spun
and hand-woven cotton dress and
scarf with embroidery and appliqué work.

BURMA (Naga tribe, upper
Chindwin River). Man's costume,
opposite, with basketry hat decorated with boar's tusks, feathers,
and fur. Loincloth is hand-woven
cotton decorated with cowrie shells.

to the primitive Buddhism of Gautama's conception. Confucianism has also had a strong hold in Southeast Asia, in keeping with the family emphasis there.

Buddhist priests are distinguished by their saffron yellow garments: robes wound loosely about the body often with one shoulder bare. Distinctions in Buddhism according to sect or place in the hierarchy are usually designated by a variety of headdresses, ornamentation, and color. Western-style pants and shirts may appear under the saffron robes, but it is the wearing of the robe proper that is necessary to the priestly office.

The usual costume of sedentary Southeast Asians falls into two main groups: in Burma, Malaysia, and much of Thailand a draped or wraparound form of costume is typical, whereas in the territories of former French Indochina the influence of China has popularized its typical combination of shirt, pants, and jacket. A delightful variation on Chinese dress is worn by young adult Vietnamese girls. This is a light, semitransparent outer garment called the *aodai*, split to the waist and worn over darker inner clothes — usually a skirt or pants. The round and peaked straw shade hat apparently of Chinese derivation is a common sight in much of Southeast Asia. Blouse and skirt combinations for women are also commonly seen, especially in Vietnam, the blouse buttoned or tied in front as in the Chinese version.

In both Vietnam and Thailand, owing to the impact of war in the former case and in part to government policy in the latter, men's traditional clothing is quickly vanishing in the river valleys. Where formerly a combination of blouse-chemise style of jacket and pants was worn in Vietnam and a blouse and wraparound or pantaloons (*sampot*) in Thailand, today Western shirts, pants, and shorts proclaim the domination of Western fashions (and ideas).

106

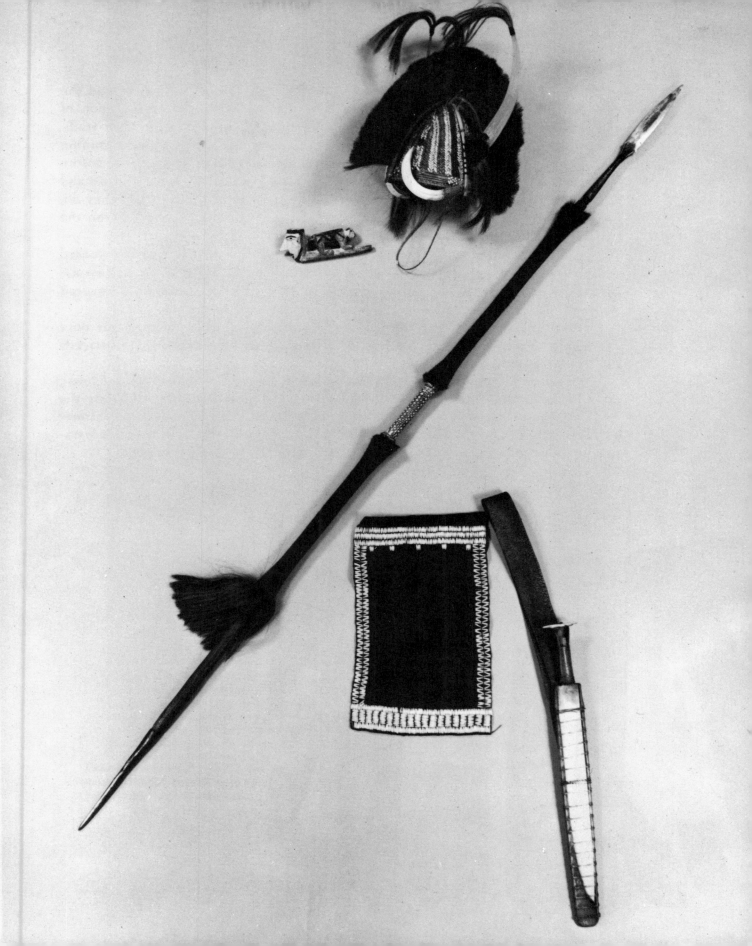

have great meaning in China. Red and gold represent happiness, wealth, prosperity, and good fortune; blue and green are feminine colors much worn by women; white is the color of wealth; yellow belongs to the emperor.

Women in the villages and shops dress in clothing similar to that of men. The cheongsam, however, of southern Chinese derivation, has been very popular both for formal wear in the villages and for everyday and formal wear in the cities. The cheongsam is a tight-fitting, sheath-like dress with upright collar, the same as in the traditional jacket. The dress falls to the lower part of the calves, but has a slit in either side between eight and ten inches long, that ends a few inches above the knee. This becoming and efficient dress is often elaborately decorated with print designs of flowers, birds, etc. Like the kimono for Japan and the sari for India, the cheongsam has served to designate the Chinese woman to the West.

Festivals and marriages have been the occasions upon which the Chinese, even the poor, lavished their resources. Pride in ancestry and in one's self as seen through the eyes of one's peers have motivated great expenditure, even to actual impoverishment. The results, of course, are dazzling, particularly for a wedding. Everyone wears the best obtainable. The profusion of silks, painted silks, satin embroideries, bird feathers and metal filigree on silk headdresses, jewelry, and both primary and delicate color is wonderful. Amid the incense smoke, the smell of good cooking, firecracker noise, and happy laughter, the modest bride reaches the groom's home in the most lavish style her family and her groom's family can manage. The beauty of the Chinese bridal gown has often attracted Western women. Those who purchase these beautiful gowns can rarely wear them, but they usually cherish them as works of art. In the end the gowns find their deserved place in museums.

Most famous of all China's costumes are the so-called "dragon robes." These were worn by members of the imperial family, by the nobility of the court, and by the Chinese gentry. The silken imperial robes of the eighteenth and nineteenth centuries were sleeved and fell full length almost to the floor. Their decoration was conventionalized and the symbols had ritual meaning. In the case of the emperor, for example, waves were depicted above the hem of the gown. Out of these grew a mountain, above which (and over the body of the gown) were clouds. Among these clouds were dragons, usually nine in number in the case of emperors, as well as such auspicious symbols as bats, cranes, flowers, and swastikas. The waves symbolized the sea, the clouds heaven, the mountain represented the earth, and the dragons the Son of Heaven, or the emperor. This total iconography would seem to mean that the emperor was the power intermediate between heaven and earth and thus relevant to both.

From the imperial robes of state and ritual descended a whole series of robes for lesser men that represented their status in the hierarchy by color and style. In

EXAMPLES OF COSTUME VARIATION WITHIN CIRCLE I:

1. Woman's dress of Sung Period
2. K'ang Hsi 12-symbol imperial robe
3. Traditional man's robe
4. Traditional woman's cheongsam
5. Man's headdress of Sung Period
6. Man's headdress of Ch'ing Dynasty

7. Man's headdress of Ch'ing Dynasty
8. Rural man
9. Rural woman
10. Woman's winter dress of north China
11. Man's winter dress of north China
12. through 15. Modern headdresses.

the case of officials this was further enhanced by a jewel or stone in the peak of their respective hats. The similarity of the officials' robes to that of the emperor represented, of course, the extension of the emperor's presence to his delegate — the mandarin.

Both Taoist and Buddhist priests had two robe repertories. One robe was plain, often austere, and worn daily to represent the simplicity of monastic or ecclesiastical life; the other was elaborate and often styled like court dress, with a different iconographic symbolism according to the ideas of the faith and the sects represented.

The Chinese theater, with its emphasis upon legend and story, is one of the most colorful of all theatrical forms and draws on the whole range of Chinese history for its costumes. The conventions of the theater are so strong, however, that the style of costume is that of traditional Chinese robes. Here the similarity ends, for the colors of makeup and gown, the accoutrement necessary for each character, and the exaggeration of symbols for dramatic purposes clearly set off theater costume from that of traditional daily life. Today, when Chinese costume on the mainland has been practically reduced to emulations of Mao Tse-tung's plain jacket and pants, to the blue uniforms of work brigades, and to the browns and grays of military and industrial life, the theater still preserves traditional color and style. Indeed, even when telling Communist legends and stories, it lends them a richness in keeping with the old tradition. The theater in China must now be more popular than ever.

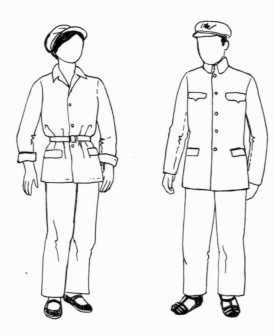

Woman's and man's costumes of People's Republic of China.

CIRCLE J:
Japan and Korea

Japan and Korea, located on the eastern flank of the Eurasian land mass, have not been isolated from the influences of other cultures. The Shosoin in Kyoto, an eighth-century treasure chamber, contains objects from Persia as well as from China, and evidence suggests that Malaysian influences reached Japan in prehistory. Both Japan and Korea are long, relatively narrow countries with the main axis of each lying along a roughly north-south line. This places the more northerly reaches of the two lands in a Siberian climatic zone, whereas the southern regions, warmed by the Japan Current, are almost tropical. Historically, then, the northern regions were open to influences from inner Asia, while the southern regions were on the sea roads to China and the south.

From at least Han times, the Koreans were the foremost sailors of eastern Asia, and it appears that Koreans carried some of the advances of Han civilization to a Japan that, because of its equitable climate and optimum subsistence situation, had been content in its isolation. After the Han period, contact with China grew steadily for both Korea and Japan. Central Asian people seem to have crossed Korea and by slow stages to have arrived at southern Japan, where they moved their military conquests northward from southern Honshu Island to the vicinity of modern Kyoto and perhaps beyond. The military emphasis these new arrivals brought to Japan established a warrior cult that was to be significant in the development of Japanese culture. Soldiers have always had a respected place in Japanese society, whereas in China the soldier had a much lower status.

In the seventh century A.D., Buddhism came to Japan; it arrived in Korea somewhat earlier than that. Its promulgation originated with the Chinese, but soon Japanese disciples traveled to China to study and to return as Buddhist missionaries. China, Korea, and Japan had old animistic faiths that tended to institutionalize in response to Buddhism's spread, and by so doing, survived into the twentieth century. Taoism in China and Shinto in Japan, for example, exist side by side with Buddhism. Confucianism became very strong in Korea but less so in Japan. Korea was partially conquered early in history by the Chinese, and by the sixteenth century the Japanese tried to conquer her as well. She always had difficulty uniting the various political entities that split the kingdom internally and frequently found herself open to attack from outside. In spite of these vulnerabilities, however, Korean culture has emerged unique and thriving.

The costumes of Korea and Japan, like those of China, vary more according

EXAMPLES OF COSTUME VARIATION WITHIN CIRCLE J:

1. Rural Japanese woman
2. Rural Japanese man
3. Traditional Japanese headdress
4. Japanese samurai headdress
5. Japanese woman
6. Traditional Japanese woman
7. Traditional Japanese man

8. Rural Korean woman
9. Rural Korean man
10. Traditional Korean woman
11. Elderly Korean man
12. Korean bride
13. Korean man
14. Korean priest

to the rank and functions of individuals or groups within society than they do as a result of regional differences. As in China, however, climatic differences influence the kind of material used to make clothing.

Korean traditional costume emphasizes the individual's stage of life. For example, Korean children of both sexes dress in bright colors, which are climaxed at marriage by the rich colors of the matrimonial pair. The bride wears a gown of silk adorned with embroidery and bright touches of red, yellow, green, and purple; on her head is a beaded crown embellished with flowers and other delicate objects. The groom wears a hat of black velvet — it is the first time he is allowed to wear any hat at all, except a shade hat in the fields — and white inner clothes covered with a bright red coat bound with a dark belt with silver buckle. After marriage, young adults wear white cotton clothes. For a man this means pants or pantaloons, a blouse, and usually a sash; women wear a white skirt fastened up high under the bosom, a white blouse tucked under the skirt, and a short jacket or bolero to complete the ensemble. The jacket may be light blue or light green. Ribbons of various colors, but rarely of prime hues, fasten over the blouse and bolero at the neckline.

Old men who have earned their retirement wear an all-white costume consisting of pantaloons, blouse, and long coat fastened by ribbons on the right side, the traditional place for fastening clothes for all ages and both sexes in Korea.

The most recognizable item in Korean clothing is the black horsehair-brimmed hat of the retired elder that, with his pipe, cane, and beard, marks his honorable status as nothing else could.

The celebrated kimono of the Japanese is one of the most versatile of all traditional forms, and variations of it are worn by both men and women. Today men wear the kimono mostly at home or at leisure, but women can still be seen on the streets of Japan in this ancient and beautiful garment. The kimono is full-sleeved and of ample dimensions; it can be worn overlapping across the front of the body (left to right) or simply open in front. It is made of silk or cotton, sometimes lined or quilted.

Most Japanese wear two kimonos, an inner one and an outer one that falls to ankle length and is drawn across the body and held by a sash. Men then put on a knee-length outer coat worn open in front. Women also wear an outer kimono, longer than the man's but not as long as the inner kimono. This is held in place by the *obi*, a sash about a foot wide and between twelve and fifteen feet long. It circles the body several times. A simple knot is formed at the back. A small cushion is tied on under the knot to lift it away from the body. The final length of the obi is arranged and tied in place with tape to form traditional puffs at the back. For foot covering both sexes wear *tabi*, or toed white stockings. The wooden *geta* or the *zori* (sandals) are not worn in the house.

Women's clothes, whether formal, festive, or informal, are usually brightly

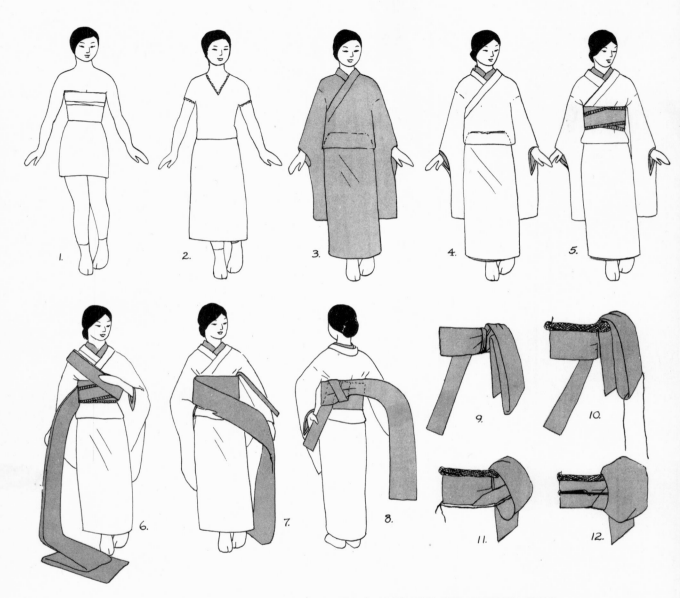

HOW TO ARRANGE THE KIMONO AND THE OBI, STEP BY STEP:

(1.) Cotton binder over breast, cotton underskirt. (2.) Cotton blouse, silk skirt. (3.) Naga juban — made one size, shortened at waist with tape or stitched tuck. (4.) Kimono — raised to individual length with cotton tape circling the waist three times. (5.) Sash — wrapped tightly to secure collar line of kimono. (6.) Obi — eleven to fourteen feet long, two feet wide, folded to eight inches wide at one end. (7.) Obi crosses the front two times. (8.) The narrow end makes a knot at the back. (9.) Obi is tightened and wide end is folded under itself. (10.) Pad is tied under fold at back and string brought through loop. (11.) Narrow end is folded in and string through loop goes around and tucks in at waist. (12.) Decorative tape tied around obi last.

KOREA. Old man's costume,
nineteenth century. Coat and
jacket are crisp silk; alternating
gauze and plain weave create a
floral pattern. Trousers are silk
damask. Hat is made of very
fine stiffened straw.

Circle J

125

JAPAN. Traditional geisha costume (opposite).
Silk outer kimono, printed with trees, leaves,
birds, and animals, is re-embroidered with silk
and metallic gold threads. Hem is padded. Sash
(obi) is of brocaded silk with pattern of musical
instruments. A detail is shown above.

KOREA. Married woman's
costume, nineteenth and early
twentieth centuries. Jacket is
crisp silk with alternating gauze
and plain weave. Apron and
trousers are of stiffened gauze.

128

JAPAN. Traditional woman's
costume. Inner and outer kimonos
are of silk with printed designs.
Sash (obi) is also silk with brocaded
blackbirds, water, and gold and
silver clouds.

colored often with fine embroidery and other delicate decorations adding to the feminine quality of the costume. The color is never more splendidly demonstrated than in the traditional wedding kimono. Men, on the other hand, appear somber in their garb of muted colors. Pants or pantaloons over the inner kimono, or simply with a blouse tied with a sash, are worn by village men and women. The sash and the obi are used as standard holders for fans, handkerchiefs, purses, and pens. The farmer's shade hat and the elaborate headdresses worn by the geisha are today almost the last of the wonderful array of headgear depicted by the paintings and prints of nineteenth-century Japan.

The costumes of the Japanese theater — in particular the extraordinary *No* theater — preserve much of the color of the court costume of pre-Meiji Japan. Much has been written on the subject, but one thing should be noted here. The No players' costumes, emulating the costumes of an older Japan, suggest that the Japanese were aware that their architecture required the correct costume if a total aesthetic picture was to be made. In other words, the adoption of the Western clothing now prevalent in Japan has destroyed a major element in the aesthetic unity conceived by the architects of the past. There is certainly a clash of values when the modern visitor, dressed for efficiency, enters buildings built for individuals dressed for beauty.

Medieval Japanese woman's dress showing obi tied in front.

130

CIRCLE K:
Southeast Siberia, Manchuria, Hokkaido, and Bonins

The region marked by the Amur River and its tributaries, the maritime coast just north of Vladivostok, and the island country of Hokkaido, Sakhalin, and the Bonins form a geographic and ethnic unity. It is an area of cold climate, with snow much of the year. This is mitigated somewhat by the warming trend of the Japan Sea in its midst and by the vast, largely coniferous forests in the hills and valleys. Fishing and hunting are primary subsistence pursuits of the indigenous population, which consists of tribal groups of Tungus speakers and old Caucasian types like the Ainu of Hokkaido. Since the Amur River region acts as a boundary between Manchuria and southeastern Siberia, Chinese and inner Asian influences are manifest in the cultures of such people as the Goldi and the Gilyak who are resident there. The Ainu, now about to be assimilated into the Japanese population, have been strongly influenced by Japanese culture for at least half a millennium.

Shamanistic in religious orientation, the people of this region believe strongly in the role of supernatural forces on the actions of man. A considerable portion of both their material culture and their yearly timetable is devoted to that body of amulets, fetishes, totems, and ritual ceremonies that, they believe, aid man in the control of the supernatural. This centuries–old control, plus optimum hunting and fishing conditions, provided a substantially secure and harmonious way of life — until civilization caused its usual disruptions. Now the old aboriginal culture is largely gone. Fortunately, a few proponents still survive, so that a reasonable record of the old way of life has been obtained.

The traditional costume of the region consists of robes and jackets made of plant fiber, cotton, or animal skin. Most typical are robes created out of fishskin — usually the salmon. These skins, after removal from the fish, are dried, then beaten, moistened, stretched, and finally smoked. The result is a tough, durable, and not unhandsome costume material. Fishskin dress has had rather universal summer and formal use in this region. The Ainu still use it for leggings, and until recently, almost all clothing was made of it by the Amur River tribes. Fascinating examples of cultural integration are shown by Goldi costumes that are essentially Chinese in form but made of fishskin instead of silk. Skins of all kinds (including dog) are made into long-sleeved fur robes and used by all the people of this region in winter, along with pants, leggings, and/or long boots.

Hats or head coverings are varied in the region. The Ainu headband, the Ainu chief's fiber crown with its carved animal, the fur hood, the Chinese shade hat, and the central Asian flap hat are typical.

The most dramatic and distinctive costume feature is the region's repertory of embroidered and sewn decoration. The designs are a combination of borrowings from Chinese and Japanese cultures added to indigenous motifs and given colorful and ingenious local character. The Ainu robes are famous for their beautiful decorations which are basically white on a blue, green, or black background. Since the kimono is emulated in the women's robes, these designs are particularly prominent on the back and lower areas of the robe. The men's traditional garb, however, is a sleeveless robe pulled over an inner garment similar to a kimono. In this case the shoulders and margins of the front openings and the hem are elaborately decorated.

The Ainu tribes exhibit an incredible combination of color and line in their Chinese-style fishskin robes and in the silk ones they have obtained from the Chinese. Study of these designs reveals iconographic as well as aesthetic reasons for the design symbols, some of which are Chinese in their expression of luck or prosperity while others relate to shamanistic and natural forces. Sewing metal ornaments, colorful stones, or other objects to both summer and winter robes is common practice in the region. Shamans may go to bizarre lengths in this regard to emphasize their concern with the supernatural.

With the exception of the especially distinctive dress of a chief, a shaman, a successful hunter, a bride, or the elderly who are privileged to wear certain designs or ornaments, the costumes within a tribal group as a whole are homogeneous and reflect its social organization.

JAPAN (Ainu, Sapporo, Hokkaido Island). Traditional chief's costume, believed to date from the sixteenth century. The coat is made of nettle cloth with cotton warp stripe. Hem and sleeves are of cotton patchwork overlay with embroidered scroll-like designs. Crown is of ohiyo bark with metal disks and a carved wooden dog.

132

JAPAN. Traditional workman's
costume. Entirely of plain weave
cotton, indigo dye. Hat is straw.

133

JAPAN. Rain clothes, also worn with snowshoes
or ice crampons in the mountains. Entire costume
is made of straw attached to a base of string
netting. Acquired in 1869, this was the first Asian
costume in the Museum's collection.

JAPAN (Ainu, Shiroi Village, Hokkaido Island). Traditional man's and woman's costumes. Coats of cotton with appliquéd cutout and overlay, re-embroidered with scroll-like designs. This ornamentation, distinctive of the Ainu, seems to be a blend of their own artistic inspiration with that of Japanese and Amur River tribes.

SIBERIA (Goldi, Amur River, Russo-Chinese border). Shaman's costume of soft skin painted with mystic symbols. The tree on one side of skirt depicts the route the shaman takes to the underworld; the other side of the skirt shows a tree he climbs to return to the earth with knowledge of where to find good hunting places. Painted animals possibly represent the game he expects to locate for his tribe.

138

SIBERIA (Goldi, Amur River, Russo-Chinese border). Bridal coats, nineteenth century, back view. Silk Chinese brocades and damasks with homespun cottons. Embroidery is both Chinese and Goldi. In their design and ornamentation these coats show a mixture of the art and workmanship of the two cultures. The Goldi-type embroidery is raised, or "couched," over bits of bark, and the hems have typical Goldi cutout and appliqué work in scroll-like designs of stylized cocks and fishes. A detail is shown on the opposite page.

SIBERIA (Goldi, Amur River, Russo-Chinese
border). Man's and woman's costumes, nineteenth
century, worn in summer. Both coats are made of
softened salmon skins. Woman's coat (right) is
painted; cutout and appliqué work on man's
costume is the more typical Goldi technique for
decorating clothing, household possessions, and
even boats. Designs are stylized cocks and fishes.
Hats are decorated birch bark.

140

EXAMPLES OF COSTUME VARIATION WITHIN CIRCLE K:

1. Goldi birchbark hat
2. Goldi traditional design
3. Back of Goldi woman's robe
4. Goldi man
5. Goldi woman

6. Gilyak woman
7. Gilyak man
8. Ainu woman
9. Ainu man

CIRCLE L:
Siberia

The vast region that includes the taiga and tundra portions of Eurasia, stretching from the Bering Sea to the Atlantic Ocean, possesses climatic extremes. Its Arctic cold weather endures eight to nine months of the year. Reindeer herding has been first in importance to most of the aboriginal peoples living there, with hunting and fishing ranking second. The Lapps in the west, the Koryak-Chukchi peoples of the east, and most of those between — Samoyed, Lamut, Yukaghir, some Yakut, and the Reindeer Tungus — depended equally on the condition and quantity of reindeer, though they utilized the reindeer in different ways. The dog, too, has been important to these northern people: he was herder, hunting companion, beast of burden, sacrificial victim, and food supplement. The reindeer, the dog, other animals of forest and tundra, stream and sea, furnished the raw materials necessary to life — and to costume. Russian and Scandinavian cloth, however, was eagerly sought in trade — especially for undergarments. The costumes of the nineteenth and early twentieth centuries, therefore, were generally a mixed bag of foreign cloth and local fur, hair, and hide. Today modern Russian dress is dominant.

The basic traditional costume of this region has been pants, boots, and a fur or hair shirt extending to the knees. A cowl and a collar of fur protected against the cold. This costume is still worn in places in winter and summer by both men and women. Variations occur in material and in decoration, and women embellish their clothes with soft furs and sewn designs; they added aprons and kerchiefs as these became available through trade.

As in Circle K, distinction within the group by costume was rare except for shamans, chiefs, or the wealthy. Between groups, however, distinction of hat type, clothing decoration, and color was often made. A chest piece of cloth, skin, wood, or metal, for example, was worn in much of Siberia from the Evenks of the Yenisei River to the Koryak of the maritime provinces. Yet the color, size, and symbols of this piece gave the individual ethnic identity. The Samoyed peoples tended to wear a pullover robe with a semiflared bottom edge usually decorated with tufts of reindeer hair, tassels or pieces of colored cloth. The Lapps emphasized bright blue as a background color, and their pointed hats "of the four winds" clearly distinguished them.

In both Circle L and Circle K, the seeming eagerness with which the ornamentation of other regions has been adopted by the aboriginal peoples may reflect a psychological need for color in an otherwise drab world. Whatever the reason,

EXAMPLES OF COSTUME VARIATION WITHIN CIRCLE L:

1. Koryak man
2. Koryak woman
3. Koryak boy
4. Koryak-Chukchi woman's interior dress
5. Chukchi man
6. Chukchi woman
7. Lapp man

8. Lapp man's "Hat of the Four Winds"
9. Lapp woman
10. Lapp woman
11. Yakut man
12. Yakut man
13. Yakut woman
14. Yakut woman

Lamut woman, Markovo, Siberia.

one of the most delightful and absorbing costume studies is that of the history and motivation for ornamentation in this region. The Siberian aboriginal costumes contain such design elements as Russian folk motifs, Eastern Orthodox Church symbols, and local animistic devices. The exigencies of the northern environment seem paradoxically to have motivated the adoption of gentle and graceful qualities in the efficient costume of the inhabitants.

The Russian conquest of Siberia, like the American migration into the West of North America, had its heroes and its villains. It appears, however, that the treatment of the local natives by the Russians was commendable compared to the horrors the Indians received from the Americans. This is why so many Siberian aboriginal groups still observe older customs, adapt Russian ideas to their own situation, and keep their identity as a people. Traditional costumes have therefore survived, and are now encouraged by the Soviet government to lend credence to the proclamation of a Union of Soviet peoples. The popular Russian literature of the day indicates a national awareness of what has always been true in northern Asia — that a great variety of peoples coexist there, each of whom have their own traditions and distinctive costumes.

144

SIBERIA (Samoyed,
Bolsheremelskaya tundra).
Bride's costume, nineteenth
century. Reindeer and wolf fur
with flannel insets and tassels.

SIBERIA (Koryak, Baron Korf's Bay). Woman's costume, nineteenth century. Reindeer skin outside, fur against body. Wolf and beaver fur trim, beadwork at hem, pendants of glass beads attached to Russian coins, buttons, and metal disks.

146

SIBERIA (Koryak). Fur undergarment, with boots, to be worn
under coat. Made of brown and
white pieced reindeer fur.

SIBERIA (Yukaghir). Shaman's costume of reindeer skin and fur, with only one metal ornament. The tassels and pendants are made of fur and bits of cotton. The cap is skin with fur pendants.

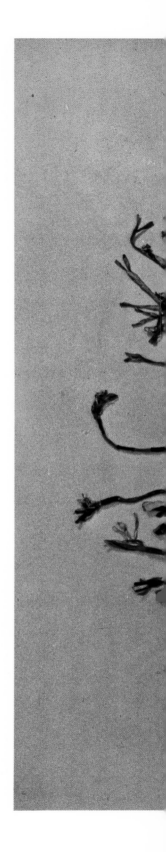

EASTERN SIBERIA (Russianized natives). Man's
costume, nineteenth and early twentieth centuries,
worn in winter. Entire costume is made of reindeer
fur; coat has an inner lining of fur as well. Fur
trousers are also worn. Embroidered flannel
hem — detail is on opposite page — shows
Russian influence.

150

Bibliography

Balt, Solryns. *Costume of Hindustan*. London: 1807.

Bănăteanu, Tancred. *Portul Popular Din Tasa Oasului (Caiete de Arta Populasa)*. Bucharest: Stat Pentru Literatura si Arta, 1957.

Batchelor, Rev. John. *The Ainu of Japan*. London: The Religious Tract Society, 1892.

Cammann, Schuyler. *China's Dragon Robes*. New York: The Ronald Press Co., 1962.

Casanowicz, I.M. *Parsee Religious Ceremonial Objects in the United States National Museum*. Proceedings of the United States National Museum, vol. 61. Washington, D.C.: Smithsonian Institution, 1922.

Clarke, Samuel R. *Among the Tribes in South-West China*. London: Morgan & Scott, 1911.

Dar, S.N. *Costumes of India and Pakistan*. Bombay: D.B. Taraporevala Sons & Co., 1969.

Dongerkery, Kamala. *The Indian Sari*. New Delhi: The All India Handicrafts Board, Ministry of Commerce & Industry, n.d.

Erben, R.B. *Abbildungen sammtlicher Geistlichen Orden männlich und Weiblichen Geschlechts in der Katholischen Kirche*. Prague: 1821.

Gibbs-Smith, Charles H. *The Fashionable Lady in the 19th Century*. London: Victoria & Albert Museum, 1960.

Hansen, Henny Harald. *Mongol Costumes*. Nationalmuseets Skrifter, Copenhagen: Gyldendalske Boghandel, Nordisk Forlag, 1950.

Hardie, Norman. *In Highest Nepal*. London: George Allen & Unwin, 1957.

Jochelson, W. *Peoples of Asiatic Russia, Memoirs*. New York: The American Museum of Natural History, 1928.

Kawakatsu, K. *Kimono*. Tourist Library, vol. 13. Tokyo: Maruzen Co., 1936.

Keith, E. and Scott Robertson, E.K. *Old Korea*. New York: Philosophical Library, 1947.

Kohler, Carl. Edited by E. Von Sichart. Translated by A.K. Dallas. *A History of Costume*. New York: G. Howard Watt, 1933.

Kretschmer, Albert. *Die Trachten der Volker*. Leipzig: 1906.

Laufer, B. *Decorative Art of the Amur Tribes, Memoirs*. New York: The American Museum of Natural History, 1902.

Laver, James. *Costumes of the Western World*. New York: Harper & Row, 1951.

Levin, M.G. and Potapov, L.P., editors. *The Peoples of Siberia*. Chicago: University of Chicago Press, 1964.

Lutz, Henry R. *Textiles & Costumes among the Peoples of the Ancient Near East*. Leipzig: J.C. Hinrichsische Buchhandlung, 1921.

Manker, Ernst. *Lapsk Kultur*. Acta Lapponica, Publication of Nordiska Museet, vol. IV. Stockholm: Hugo Gebers Forlag, 1944.

Markov, Joseph. *The Slovak National Dress through the Centuries*. Prague: Artia, 1956.

Marshal, Rev. H.I. *The Karen People of Burma*. London: Longmans, Green & Co., 1945.

Olufsen, O. *The Emir of Bokhara and His Country*. London: William Heinemann, 1911.

Payne, Blanche. *History of Costume*. New York: Harper & Row, 1965.

Ronaldshay, Earl of. *Lands of the Thunderbolt*. London: Constable & Co., 1923.

Rubens, Alfred. *A History of Jewish Costume*. New York: Funk & Wagnalls, 1967.

Sieroshevski, V.L. *Yakut*. Saint Petersburg: Opyt Etnograficheskago Izsliedovaniia; 1896.

Stein, Lothar. *Beduinen*. Leipzig: Museum für Völkerkunde, 1968.

Tilke, Max. *Oriental Costumes*. New York: Brentanos, 1924.

Tilke, Max. *The Costumes of Eastern Europe*. New York: E. Weyhe, 1925.

Vilkuna, Kustaa. Mannerheim's Collection of Sart Specimens. *In* C.G. Mannerheim, *Across Asia from West to East in 1906-1908*. Netherlands: Anthropological Publications, 1969. 2nd Edition.

Wilcox, R. Turner. *Folk and Festival Costume of the World*. New York: Charles Scribner's Sons, 1965.

Wilcox, R. Turner. *The Mode in Costume*. New York: Charles Scribner's Sons, 1958.

Index

Page numbers in italic indicate illustrations.

Aba. *see* Coats
Afghanistan. *see* Circle C *and* Circle D
Agal. *see* Headcoverings
Ainu tribes. *see* Circle K
Albania. *see* Circle A
American Indian, 18, 30, 144
American Museum of Natural History,
   The, 7-13
   ceremonies for opening of, *6*
   Dentan collection at, 10
   Eurasian costumes exhibit at, 11
   Fürer-Hamendorf collection at, 10
   Hall of Prehistoric Man at, 9
   Hall of Tribal Life of North Pacific
      America at, 8
   Okada collection at, 10
Amur River tribes. *see* Circle K
Andrews, Roy Chapman, 9
Animism, 90, 105, 121, 144
Aodai. *see* Dresses
Arabs. *see* Circle B *and* Circle C
Armenians. *see* Circle A *and* Circle C
Asia
   cultural features of, 31, 35
   Buddhism in, 35
   Confucianism in, 35
   development of Japanese civilization
      in, 35
   early civilization of China in, 34
   early civilization of Crete in, 35
   early civilization of Egypt in, 35
   early Sumerian civilization in, 34
   Hinduism in, 35
   Islam in, 35, 36
   "Mother Asia" mystique in, 9
Azerbaijani tribes. *see* Circle C

Bacon, Elizabeth, 40
Baktiari tribes. *see* Circle C
Balkans. *see* Circle A
Baluch tribes. *see* Circle C
Banjara tribes. *see* Circle E
Barracan. *see* Draped costumes
Batik. *see* Dyes
Bedouins. *see* Circle B
Benares. *see* Circle E
Bethlehem style. *see* Circle B
Bhutan. *see* Circle F
Blouses
   choli, 86, *89*
   entari, 49
Boas, Franz, 7-11
Bogoras, W., 8, 10
Bonins. *see.* Circle K

Brahmins. *see* Circle E
Buddhism, 35, 90, 101, 105, 106, 120,
   121
Bukhara. *see* Circle D
Burka. *see* Robes
Burma. *see* Circle H
Burnooses. *see* Robes
Buryat tribes. *see* Circle D

Caftan. *see* Robes
Cambodia. *see* Circle H
Caste. *see* Circle E
Caucasus. *see* Circle A
Chadan. *see* Coats
Chalwar. *see* Pantaloons
Cheongsam. *see* Dresses
Chinese-style dress
   in Circle F, 90
   in Circle G, 103
   in Circle H, *108, 109*
   in Circle K, 132
Choli. *see* Blouses
Chu'an Miao tribe. *see* Circle H
Chukchi tribes. *see* Circle L
Chupa. *see* Robes
Circle A: Balkans, Caucasus, and
   Ukraine
   Albanians of, 49
   anthropological studies in Serbia
      in, 10
   Armenians of, 49, 51
   boundaries of, 49
   bullet-pouched coat of, *44,* 51
   caftan of, 49, 51
   Caucasian boots of, 51
   Caucasian hats of, 51
   Caucasian headdresses of, 51
   Central Serbian woman's costume
      of, *46*
   chalwar of, 49
   climate of, 49
   Cossack costumes of, *50,* 51
   costumes of the evzone of, 49
   costume variations within, 50
   cultural foundations of, 49
   embroidery and decoration of, *41,
      42-43, 45, 46, 47, 48,* 51
   entari of, 49
   ethnohistory of, 49
   evzone of, 49
   fez of, 49, 51
   fustanella of, 49
   Georgian costumes of, *44,* 51
   Greek costumes of, *48, 49, 50*

Herzegovinian costumes of, *50*
Hungarian costumes of, *50, 51*
jewelry of, 41
Kurds of, 49
Macedonian woman's costume of,
   42-43
Museum collections from Turkey
   in, 10
pantaloons of, 49, 51
Phrygian cap of, 49
Romanian costumes of, 51, 52
Russian woman's costume of, *50*
Southern Macedonian costumes of,
   41, 47
tarboosh of, 51
traditional Turko-Caucasian sword
   of, *50*
Transylvanian costumes of, 51
Turkish costumes of, *45,* 49, *50,* 51
Turko-Caucasian boots of, *50*
Ukrainian-Caucasian man's costume
   of, *50*
Ukrainian woman's costume of, *50*
veils of, 49, 51
vests of, *41, 47,* 49
Western dress in, 52
yashmak of, 49
Circle B: Near East
   aba of, 55, *60*
   agal of, 55, *60*
   Arab costumes of 52, *54,* 55, 56,
      59, 60
   barracan of, 55
   Bedouin costumes of, 53, *54,* 55, 56
   Bethlehem style in, 56, *59*
   boundaries of, 52
   caftan of, 55
   costumes of Sinai desert in, *54*
   costumes of Iraq in, *54, 61*
   costumes of the Levant in, 56
   costumes of Syria in, *54, 55, 57, 58,
      62*
   costume variations within, 54
   Damascus style in, 56
   dresses of, 56, *57, 59, 62*
   embroidery of, 56, *57, 59, 61, 62*
   fez of, *53, 58*
   galabia of, 55
   gandoura of, 56
   headcoverings of Arab women of,
      56, *57, 59*
   headdresses of, 55, 56, *60*
   Islam in, 53
   Israel in, 53, 56

Jerusalem style in, 56
jewelry of, 56, 57
kaffiyeh of, 55, 60
kamis of, 55
khalak of, 52
Lebanese sheik's costume of, 53
Museum collections from Arabia in, 10
Palestinian woman's costume of, 54
purdah in, 55
sandals of the Bedouin of, 55
Syrian bride's costume of, 57
shatweh of, 56
shoes of the Bedouin of, 55
tarboosh of, 56
veils of, 55, 56
Western dress in, 53, 56
yashmak of, 56
Yemenite costumes of, 54
Circle C: Iran (Persia) and Afghanistan
anthropological studies in, 10
Arabs of, 71
Armenians of, 71
Azerbaijani tribes of, 71
Baktiari tribes of, 71
Baluch tribes of, 71
burka of, 72
chadan of, 72
costume of Hazaran man of, 65
costume of Kashgai man of, 70
costume variations within, 70
costumes of Afghanistan in, 64, 65, 68, 70, 71, 72
costumes of the Baluch of, 63, 70
costumes of Iran in, 63, 66, 67, 70, 71, 72
costumes of the Pathans of, 64, 70, 86
costumes of the Pushtins of, 68, 70
costumes of West Pakistan in, 63, 71
costumes of western Turkestan in, 71
costumes of the Uzbek of, 68, 70
cultural features of, 69, 71
dresses of, 63, 67, 72
embroidery of, 55, 63, 64, 65, 66, 67, 71, 72
Hazaran tribes of, 71
headpieces of Afghan women of, 72
Islam in, 71
Kashgai tribes of, 71
Kirghiz tribes of, 71
kola of, 68, 71, 72
Lurs of, 71
mirror work of, 71
modern conformity of dress in Iran in, 28
Museum collections from, 10
pantaloons of, 71, 72
Pathan tribes of, 71
purdah in, 71

purdah costume of, 72
pushtin of, 64, 71
Pushtin tribes of, 71
Safi tribes of, 68
shoes of Afghanistan in, 72
Tajik tribes of, 71
tombon of, 71
turbans of, 70, 71
Turkmen of, 71
Uzbek tribes of, 71
veil of Afghanistan in, 72
vests of, 64, 71, 72
waistcoats of, 71, 72
Circle D: Central Asia
boundaries of, 73
boots of, 73
caftan of, 73
costume of Bukhara in, 77
costume variations within, 74
costumes of the Buryat of, 73
costumes of Kazakstan in, 73, 74
costumes of Kirgizia in, 73
costumes of eastern Manchuria in, 73
costumes of Mongolian territories in, 73, 74, 80
costumes of north Afghanistan in, 75, 78
costumes of Tadzhikistan in, 73
costumes of Turkmen of, 73, 74, 75, 78
costumes of Uzbekistan in, 73, 74
costumes of the Yakut of, 73, 79
del of, 73
dolman of, 73
dresses of, 77, 78
embroidery of, 73 77, 78, 79
hats of the Mongols of, 75
hats of the Turkmen of, 75
headdresses of the Mongols of, 74, 75
how to tie a turban of, 76
ikat of, 73, 77
jewelry of, 75, 76, 78, 79
kola of, 73
kurta of, 78
monk's costume of Mongolia in, 80
nomads of, 73
Persian-style dress in, 73
Tartar hat of, 75
turban of, 73, 76
tyubeterka of, 75
Circle E: India and Pakistan
anthropological studies in Pakistan in, 10
Benares sari cloth of, 38, 86
caste in, 88
choli of, 86
costume of Banjara woman of, 83
costume cloth of, 88
costume of Punjabi woman of, 87
costume of Sindi woman of, 84

costume variations within, 87
costumes of Brahmins of, 88
costumes of Jains of, 88
costumes of Parsees of, 88
costumes of Rabari tribe of, 82
costumes of Rajasthan of, 87, 88
costumes of Sikhs of, 87, 88
dhoti of, 86
dupatta of, 85
dyes of, 88
embroidery of, 81, 82, 83, 84
Gandhi cloth cap of, 86
how to drape a sari of, 89
jewelry of, 83
kola of, 86
mirror work decoration of, 82, 83, 88
modern conformity of dress in, 28
Museum collections from, 10
"Nehru"-style dress of, 87
Orissan costume cloth of, 88
paisley samples of, 81
Persian-style costume in, 85
sari of, 81, 86, 87, 89
shalwa-kamis of, 85
Western clothing in, 88
woodblock-printing in, 88
"Zone of Attraction" of, 85, 86, 88
"Zone of Isolation" of, 85, 88
"Zone of Relative Attraction" of, 85, 86, 88
Circle F: The High Borderlands — Kashmir, Nepal, Sikkim, and Bhutan
animism in, 90
Buddhism in, 90
Chinese mandarin-style in, 90
costume of Lepcha man from Sikkim, of, 91
costume of Sherpa woman from Nepal, of, 91
costume and social rank in, 90
costume variation within, 91
costumes of Bhutan in, 90, 91, 96
costumes of Nepal in, 90, 91, 93, 97
costumes of Kashmir in, 90, 92, 95
costumes of Sikkim in, 90, 91
dhoti of, 90
dyes of, 93
embroidery and decoration of, 93, 95, 96, 97
geography of, 90
Hinduism in, 90
Islam in, 90
Kashmiri hat of, 92, 95
Kashmiri shawl of, 92
Lepchas of, 90
Museum collections from Nepal in, 10
Nepalese woman's headdress of, 93
robes of, 90, 92
sari of, 90
shalwa-kamis of, 92

Shembas of, 90
Sherpas of Nepal in, 90
Tibetan-style dress in, 90
vests of, 92
weaving in Kashmir in, 92
Circle G: Tibet
anthropological studies in, 10, 11
boots of, *98*
Buddhism in, 101
Chinese robes of, *100*, 103
chupa of, *98, 99*, 103
costume of shaman of, *102*
costume variation with, *102*
costume of yellow-hat lama of, *102*
costumes of the monks in, *100*, 101, *102*
costumes of the nobility in, *102*, 103
costumes of the nomads of, *99, 102*, 103
costumes of the peasants of, *102*, 103
cultural features of, 101
Dalai Lama of, 101
dyes of, *99*
embroidery and decoration of, *98, 99, 100*, 103
geography of, 101
hats of, *98, 99*, 103
headdresses of, *98, 102*
jewelry of, *98*, 103
Museum collections from, 11
Red China and, 101
robes of, 101, 103
regional differences of, 101, 103
Circle H: Southeast Asia
animism in, 105
anthropological studies in Laos in, 10
aodai of, 106
batik of, *109*
boundaries of, 105
Buddhism in, 105, 106
Burmese headdresses of, *112*
cheongsam of, 108
Chinese style in, 106, *108, 109*
Confucianism in, 106
costume variation within, *104*
costumes of Buddhist priests in, 106, *111*
costumes of Burma in, 106, *107*, 108, *111, 112*
costumes of Cambodia in, *104*, 106
costumes of Chinese Chu'an Miao tribe of, *108, 109*
costumes of Laos in, *104, 110*
costumes of Malaysia in, *104*, 106
costumes of Thailand in, *104*, 106
costumes of Vietnam in, *104*, 106
cultural features of, 105
dyes of, 105
embroidery and decorations of, 106, *107, 108, 109, 110, 112*
fez of, 108

Hinduism in, 105
Islam in, 105
jewelry of, 105
lungi of, 108, *111, 112*
Museum collections from, 10
pillbox hat of, 108
sampet of, 108
sampot of, 106
sari of, 108
sarong of, 108
shade hats of, 106, *107, 109*
tarboosh of, 108
turban of, 108
western dress in, 106
Circle I: China
ancestor cult of, 117
bridal gown of, 118
Buddhism in, 120
cheongsam of, 118, *119*
clogs of, 117
Confucianism in, 117
costume and social rank in, 117
costume of unmarried girl of, *113*
costume variations within, *119*
costumes of People's Republic of China, *120*
costumes of theater of, *114, 115*, 120
cultural features of, 117
"dragon robes" of, *115*, 118
embroidery and decoration of, *113, 114, 115, 116*, 118
festival clothes of, 118
headdresses of, *119*
K'ang Hsi 12-symbol imperial robe of, *119*
Laufer's expedition to, 9
man's and boy's winter wear of, *116*
Manchus of, 117
mandarin dress in, *115* 120
modern dress and conformity in, 28
Mongols of, 117
Museum collections from, 10
priests' robes in, 120
slippers of, 117
skull cap of, 117
Taoism in, 120
Tibetans of, 117
Turks of, 117
waistcoats of, 117
winter dress of, *116, 119*
Circle J: Japan and Korea
animism in, 121
Buddhism in, 121
Confucianism in, 121
costume of the geisha of, *127*, 130
costume and social rank in, 121
costume variations within, *122*
cultural influences on, 121
embroidery and decoration of, 123, *125, 127, 128*, 130
geta of, 123

how to arrange the kimono and obi of, *124*
Japanese headdress of, *122*
Japanese rain clothes of, *134-135*
Japanese Samurai headdress of, *122*
Japanese theatrical costumes of, 130
Japanese medieval woman's costume of, *130*
Japanese No theater of, 130
Japanese woman's costume of, *129*
Japanese workman's costume of, *133*
Japanese wedding kimono of, 130
kimono of, 123, *124, 127, 129, 130*
Korean bride's dress of, *122*
Korean child's dress of, 123
Korean groom's hat of, 123
Korean priest's dress of, *122*
Korean elder's dress of, 19, *122, 123, 125*
Korean retired elder's hat of, 123, *125*
Korean wedding dress of, 123
Korean married woman's costume of, *128*
Korean young adult's dress of, 123
Museum collections from Japan in, 10
obi of, 123, *124, 127, 129, 130*
pantaloons of, 123, 130
Shinto in, 121
tabi of, 123
warrior cult of Japan in, 121
Western dress in, *26*, 130
zori of, 123
Circle K: Southeast Siberia, Manchuria, Hokkaido, and Bonins
Amur River tribes of, 9, 131
anthropological studies among Ainu, Gilyak, and Goldi of, 9
boots of, 131
crown of Ainu chief of, *132*
Chinese style in, 132
climate of, 131
costume of Ainu chief of, *132*
costume variations within, *141*
costumes of Ainu tribes of, 131, *132, 136, 141*
costumes of Gilyak tribes of, *141*
costumes of Goldi tribes of, 131, *137 138-139, 140, 141*
embroidery of, *132, 136, 137, 138-139, 140*
geography of, 131
headband of Ainu of, 131
Goldi birchbark hat of, *141*
Goldi bridal coat of, *138-139*
fishskin dress of, 131, 132, *140*
fur robes of, 131
hoods of, 132
Japanese style in, 132
leggings of, 131

157

shaman's costume of, *137*
shamanism in, 131, 132
Circle L: Siberia
animism in, 144
chest pieces of, 142
climate of, 142
costume variations within, *143*
costume of Yukaghir shaman of, *148-149*
costumes of the Chukchi tribes of, 142, *143*
costumes of the Evenks of, 142
costumes of the Koryak tribes of, 142, *143, 147, 152*
costumes of the Koryak-Chukchi tribes of, 142, *143*
costumes of the Lamut tribes of, 142, *144*
costumes of the Lapps of, 142, *143, 146*
costumes of Reindeer Tungus tribes of, 142
costume of Russianized man of, *150-151*
costumes of Samoyed tribes of, 142, *145*
costumes of the Yakut tribes of, 142, *143*
embroidery and decoration of, 142, 144, 145, 146, *148-149, 150-151, 152*
Koryak boots of, *147*
Lapp boots of, *146*
Lapp hat "of the four winds" of, 142, *143*
Museum collections from, 10
reindeer herding in, 142
and Soviet Union, 144
use of reindeer skin in, 142, *148-149*
use of reindeer fur in, 142, *145, 146, 147, 148, 149, 150-151, 152*
Circles of ethnohistory, 40
see also Circles A through L
Clogs. *see* Footwear
Coats
aba, 55, *60*
Caucasian bullet-pouched, 44, 51
chadan, 72
pushtin, *64, 71*
Confucianism, 35, 106, 117, 121
Cossacks. *see* Circle A
Costume
and architecture, 28
and attitudes toward sexuality, 20, 21, 29
and behavioral attitudes, 16
and culture, 13
and effect on character, 20, 29
as an expression of identity, 19, 21, 28, 29
the "great tradition" of, in Asia, 37, 38

the "great tradition" of, in Europe, 37, 38
the "little" or folk tradition of, in Asia, 37
the "little" or folk tradition of, in Europe, 37, 38
and modern industrialization, 14
and social rank, 90, 117, 121
and status, 19, 21, 29
Cotton
early cultivation of, 22
Cultural zones of Eurasia, *see* Circles of Ethnohistory
Cutting, Sudyam, 10

Dalai Lama, 11, 101
Damascus style, *see* Circle B
Del. *see* Robes
Dhoti. *see* Draped costumes
Dolman. *see* Robes
"Dragon robe". *see* Robes
Draped costumes
barracan, 55
dhoti, 86, 90
early use of, 22
lungi, 108, *111, 112*
method of draping sari, *89*
prejudice against, 23
sari, 24, 29, 38, *81, 86, 87, 89,* 90, 108, 118
sarong, 108
sampet, 108
Dresses
of Afghanistan and Iran, *63, 67, 72*
aodai, 106
of Central Asia, 77, 78
cheongsam, 108, 118, *119*
Chinese bridal gown, 118
of Iran, *63,* 72
kurta, *78*
of Near East, 56, 57, 59, 62
of Thai bride, *106*
Dupatta. *see* Headcoverings
Dupree, Louis, 10
Dyes
batik, *109*
early use of, 21
ikat, 73, 77
of India, 88
of Nepal, 93
of Southeast Asia, 105
of Tibet, *93,* 99
woodblock-printing, 30, 88

Embroidery and decoration
of Afghanistan, *64, 65,* 71, 72
of the Ainu, *132, 136*
of Bhutan, *96*
of Central Asia, 73, 77, 78, 79
of China, *113, 114, 115, 116,* 118
Chinese style of, among the Goldi, *138-139*

of the Goldi, *137, 138-139,* 140
"graphta," in Greece, 48
of India, *81, 82, 83*
of Iran, *63, 66,* 71
of Japan, 123, *127,* 130
of Kashmir, 95
of Korea, *125, 128*
of Macedonia, 41, *42-43, 47*
of Near East, 56, 57, 59, *61, 62*
of Nepal, *93, 97*
of Serbia, 46
of Siberia, 142, 144, *145, 146, 148-149, 150-151, 152*
of Southeast Asia, *106, 107, 108, 109, 110, 112*
of Tibet, 98, 99, 100, *103*
of Turkey, 45
of West Pakistan, *84*
Entari. *see* Blouses
Erin, Kenan, 10
Ethnohistory. *see* Circles of ethnohistory
Eurasia
beginnings of civilization in, 21
and conflict between Islam and Christianity, 36
development of civilization in, 34-35
Eastern civilization in, 35
physical features of, 34
Western civilization in, 35
Europe
Christianity in, 35-36
cultural features of, 31, 35
early Roman civilization in, 35
Evenks. *see* Circle L
Evzone. *see* Circle A

Fez. *see* Headcoverings
Folk order. *see* "Little tradition"
Footwear
Bedouin sandals, 55
Bedouin shoes, 55
Caucasian boots, 51
Central Asian boots, 73
Chinese slippers, 117
clogs, 117
geta, 123
Koryak boots, *147*
Lapp boots, *146*
of Afghanistan, 72
Southeast Siberian boots, 131
tabi, 123
Tibetan boots, *98*
Turko-Caucasian boots, *50*
zori, 123
Fustanella. *see* Circle A

Galabia. *see* Shirts
Gandoura. *see* Robes
Gandhi cloth cap. *see* Headcoverings
Geisha. *see* Circle J
Georgia. *see* Circle A

158

Geta. *see* Footwear
Gilyak tribes. *see* Circle K
Gobi Desert expeditions, 9
Godey's *Ladies' Book*, 13
Goldi tribes. *see* Circle K
Gordon, A. K., 10
"Great tradition", The
  and the Christian church, 25
  definition of, 23
  and the military, 25
  rapid change within, 24
  and the robes of Judaism, 25
  style-consciousness of, 24
  and the Western theater, 25
"Graphta." *see* Embroidery and decoration
Greece. *see* Circle A

Halpern, Joel, 10
Hats. *see* Headcoverings
Hazara. *see* Circle C
Headcoverings. *see also* Headdresses
  agal, 55, *60*
  Ainu headband, 131
  basketry hat of Chu'an Miao tribe, *107, 109*
  Caucasian hats, 51
  Cossack hats, 51
  crown of Ainu chief, *132*
  dupatta, 85
  fedora, 117
  fez, 30, 49, 51, *53, 58*, 108
  fur hood, 132
  Gandhi cloth cap, 86
  Goldi birchbark hat, *141*
  hats of the Mongols, 75
  Hats of the Turkmen, 75
  Japanese rain hat, *134-135*
  kaffiyeh, 55, *60*
  Kashmiri hat, 92, *95*
  khalak, 52
  kola, *68*, 71, 72, 73, 86
  Korean groom's hat, 123
  Korean retired elder's hat, 123, *125*
  Lapp hat, 142, *143*
  Phrygian cap, 49
  pillbox, 108
  shatweh, 56
  skull cap, 117
  straw shade hat, 106, 117, 123, 130
  tarboosh, 51, 56, 108
  Tartar hat, 24, 38, 75
  Tibetan hats, *98, 99*, 103
  turban, 24, 38, *70*, 71, 73, *76*, 108
  tyubeterka, 75
Headdresses
  of Afghan women, 72
  of Arab women, 56, 57, *59*
  of Burma, *112*
  of Caucasus, 51
  of China, Ch'ing Dynasty, *119*
  of China, modern, *119*

  of China, Sung Period, *119*
  of Japan, the geisha, 130
  of Japan, the samurai, *122*
  of Japan, traditional, *122*
  of Mongols, *74, 75*
  of Near East, 55, 56, *60*
  of Nepalese women, *93*
  of Tibetan women, *98, 102*
  of Tibetan men, *102*
Herzegovinia. *see* Circle A
Hinduism, 35, 90, 105
Hokkaido. *see* Circle K
How to arrange kimono and obi, *124*
How to drape sari, *89*
How to tie turban, *76*
Hungary. *see* Circle A

Ikat. *see* Dye
Indonesia, 105
Iran. *see* Circle C
Iraq. *see* Circle B
Islam, 35, 36, 53, 71, 90, 105
Israel. *see* Circle B

Jacobsen, Vladimir, 8, 10
Jains. *see* Circle E
Jerusalem style. *see* Circle B
Jesup, Morris K., 8, 10
Jewelry
  of Banjara tribe, *83*
  of Central Asia, 75, 76, *78, 79*
  of Near East, 56, *57*
  of Southeast Asia, 105
  of Southern Macedonia, *41*
  of Tibet, *98*, 103

Kaffiyeh. *see* Headcoverings
Kamis. *see* Shirts
Kashgai tribes. *see* Circle C
Kashmiri. *see* Circle F
Kashmiri shawl. *see* Circle F
Kazakstan. *see* Central Asia
Khalak. *see* Headcoverings
Kirghiz tribes. *see* Circle C
Kirgizia. *see* Circle D
Kimono. *see* Robes
Kola. *see* Headcoverings
Korea. *see* Circle J
Koryak tribes. *see* Circle L
Koryak-Chukchi tribes. *see* Circle L
Krader, Lawrence, 10
Kurds. *see* Circle A
Kurta. *see* Dresses

Lamut tribes. *see* Circle L
Laos. *see* Circle H
Lapps. *see* Circle L
Laufer, Berthold, 8-10
Lebanon. *see* Circle B
Lepchas. *see* Circle F
Levant, the. *see* Circle B
"Little tradition", The

  of Asia, 37
  effects of industrialization on, 28
  effects of mass media on, 28
  effects of national states on, 28
  of Europe, 23
  lack of change within, 25
  personal and traditional quality of, 24
Lungi. *see* Draped costumes
Lurs. *see* Circle C

Macedonia. *see* Circle A
Malaysia. *see* Circle H
Manchuria. *see* Circle D and Circle K
Manchus. *see* Circle I
Mandarin. *see* Circle I
Mao Tse-tung, 31, 120
Marxism, 36
Menchner, Joan, 10
Middle East. *see* Circle B
Mongolia. *see* Circle D
Mongols. *see* Circle D *and* Circle I
Mustafa Kemal, 49

Nelson, N. C., 9
"Nehru"-style dress. *see* Circle E
Nepal. *see* Circle F
No theater. *see* Circle J
Nomads
  of Central Asia, 73
  of Tibet, *99, 102, 103*
Norbu, Thubten, 11

Obi. *see* Circle J
Osborn, Henry Fairfield, 9

Paisley. *see* Circle E
Pakistan. *see* Circle E
Palestine. *see* Circle B
Pantaloons
  of Afghanistan 71, 72
  chalwar, 49
  of Iran, 71, 72
  of Japan, 130
  of Korea, 123
  sampot, 106
  shalwa-kamis, 85, 92
  tombon, 71
Parsees. *see* Circle E
Pathans tribes. *see* Circle C
People's Republic of China. *see* Circle I
Persia. *see* Circle C
Persian-style dress
  in Central Asia, 73
  in India and Pakistan, 85
Punjab. *see* Circle E
Purdah, 55, 71, *72*
Pushtin. *see* Coats
Pushtin tribes. *see* Circle C

Rabari tribes. *see* Circle E
Rajasthan, 87, 88
Reindeer Tungus tribes. *see* Circle L

Robes
  burka, 72
  burnoose, 24
  caftan, 38, 49, 51, 55, 73
  Chinese, 103, 118, *119*, 120
  chupa, *98, 99,* 103
  del, 73
  dolman, 73
  "dragon robe", *115,* 118
  fishskin robes, 131
  fur robes, 131
  gandoura, 56
  Goldi woman's robe, *141*
  kimono, 38, 118, 123, *127, 129*
Romania. *see* Circle A
Russia. *see* Circle A
Safi tribes. *see* Circle C
Samoyed tribes. *see* Circle L
Sampet. *see* Draped costumes
Sampot. *see* Pantaloons
Samurai. *see* Circle J
Sandals. *see* Footwear
Sari. *see* Draped costumes
Sarong. *see* Draped costumes
Shalwa-kamis. *see* Pantaloons
Shamanism. *see* Circle K
Shapiro, Harry L., 9, 10
Shatweh. *see* Headcoverings
Shembas. *see* Circle F
Sherpas. *see* Circle F
Shinto. *see* Circle J
Shirts
  galabia, 55
  kamis, 55
Shoes. *see* Footwear
Sikhs. *see* Circle E
Sikkim. *see* Circle F
Silk
  early use of, 22
  prejudice against, 23
Sinai desert. *see* Circle B

Sind. *see* Circle E
Skull cap. *see* Headcoverings
Slippers. *see* Footwear
Soviet Union, 30, 144
Southern Macedonia. *see* Circle A
Subbarao, B., 85
Syria. *see* Circle B

Tabi. *see* Footwear
Tadzhikistan. *see* Circle D
Tailored clothing
  early use of, 22
  prejudice against, 23
Tajik. *see* Circle C
Taoism. *see* Circle I
Tarboosh. *see* Headcoverings
Tartar hat. *see* Headcoverings
Thailand. *see* Circle H
Theatrical costumes
  of China, *114,* 120
  of Japan, 130
  of the West, 25
Tibet. *see* Circle G
Tibetans. *see* Circles F, G *and* I
Tibetan-style dress. *see* Circles F, G *and* I
Tombon. *see* Pantaloons
Transylvania. *see* Circle A
Turkestan. *see* Circle C
Turkmen. *see* Circle C *and* Circle D
Turkmenistan. *see* Circle C
Turks. *see* Circle A *and* Circle I
Turban. *see* Headcoverings
Turkey. *see* Circle A
Tyubeterka. *see* Headcoverings

Ukraine. *see* Circle A
Uzbekistan. *see* Circle D
Uzbek tribes. *see* Circle C *and* Circle D

Veils, 49, 51, 56, *72*
  see also Yashmak

Vests, *41, 47, 49, 55, 58, 64, 71, 72,* 92
Vietnam. *see* Circle H

Waistcoats, *71, 117*
Weaving, development of, 21
West Pakistan. *see* Circle C *and* Circle E
Western dress
  in Asia, 14, 28, 30
  and blacks in America, 19
  color in, 17
  conformity in, 14, 15, 16, 17, 18, 28
  in Eastern Europe, 52
  and European folk tradition, 18
  fads in, 17
  and the fashion elite, 17
  in India and Pakistan, 88
  in Japan, 26, 130
  and the mass media, 18
  and the mortality of culture, 30
  in the Near East, 56
  and occupational differences, 15
  rapid change in, 16, 23, 24, *26-27*
  and social differences, 15
  and the Soviet Union, 30
  in Southeast Asia, 106
  and the youth revolt, 14
Woodblock-printing. *see* Dyes
Wool
  genesis of, 22
  prejudice against, 22

Yakut tribes. *see* Circle D *and* Circle L
Yashmak. *see* Veils
Yemenites. *see* Circle B
Yukaghir tribes. *see* Circle L

"Zone of Attraction." *see* Circle E
"Zone of Isolation." *see* Circle E
"Zone of Relative Attraction." *see* Circle E
Zori. *see* Footwear

Additional Photographic Credits

The American Museum of Natural History: pages 6, 27, 32, 33, 36, 37, 144.
Frederick Lewis Photographs: page 15.
Fred Stimpson: pages 60, 98
UPI: page 12.

The Author

Dr. Walter A. Fairservis, Jr. is a Research Associate in the Department of Anthropology at The American Museum of Natural History in addition to being Chairman of the Department of Anthropology and Sociology at Vassar College. His previous books include *Cave Paintings of the Great Hunters*, *The Origins of Oriental Civilization*, and *The Roots of Ancient India*.